MESSENGERS OF LIGHT

The Angels' Guide to Spiritual Growth

MESSENGERS OF LIGHT

The Angels' Guide to Spiritual Growth

Terry Lynn Taylor

H J Kramer Inc
Tiburon, California

Published by H J Kramer Inc.
P.O. Box 1082
Tiburon, CA 94920

Editor: Nancy Grimley Carleton
Cover Art and Design: Francesca Angelesco
Typesetting: Classic Typography
Book Production: Schuettge & Carleton

Manufactured in the United States of America
10 9 8 7 6 5 4 3 2

Library of Congress Cataloging-in-Publication Data

Taylor, Terry Lynn, 1955–
  Messengers of light: the angels' guide to spiritual
growth/by Terry Lynn Taylor.
    p.   cm.
  Includes bibliographical references.
  ISBN 0-915811-20-0 : $9.95
  1. Angels.   I. Title.
  BL477.T39   1989   89-92333
  291.2'15—dc20   CIP

Angels can fly because they take themselves lightly.

G.K. Chesterton

To Our Readers

The books we publish are our contribution to an emerging world based on cooperation rather than on competition, on affirmation of the human spirit rather than on self-doubt, and on the certainty that all humanity is connected. Our goal is to touch as many lives as possible with a message of hope for a better world.

Hal and Linda Kramer, Publishers

Contents

Foreword

When I first met Terry Taylor and heard about all of her remarkable angel experiences, I was a bit envious. I wanted an angel experience, too.

Every night before I went to bed, I'd send out a mental prayer fax requesting my very own bona fide angel experience. "Okay, highest angel. If you're really there, prove it. I want to meet an angel. ASAP. Thanks, hon."

I figured it was all right to be blunt because, as Terry assured me, angels appreciate a no-nonsense approach to things. They also have a great sense of humor, which I hoped they weren't indulging at my expense as the weeks passed and the only remotely heavenly visitation I received was a house call from two effervescent Jehovah's Witnesses. I dispensed of these hefty ladies quickly enough, although the guilty thought did occur to me that they might very well have been angels in disguise and I'd really screwed up.

"Don't worry about it," Terry would laugh. "You'll have an angel experience one of these days. Just be patient."

Several weeks later, I was sitting in a coffee shop in Silverlake, writing away, when a round, jolly, bearded young man in a loud Hawaiian shirt waved to me from another table.

"You look like the kind of person who'd like to see something wonderful that I just bought!" he trilled.

"Sure," I replied.

He trotted over to my table with a big bag, from which he produced the most beautiful carved stone cherub head I'd ever seen.

"Oh!" I breathed. "I've been wanting one of these for at least a year!"

"Would you like it?" he smiled.

"Would I! I mean . . ." I looked at him keenly. "How much is it?"

"I'll sell it to you for twelve dollars."

I knew that this was a fabulous bargain because I'd just been to Bullock's, where tacky-looking terra-cotta cherubs were going for thirty-five bucks.

"It's a deal!" I grabbed the cherub. "Who are you?"

My new friend shrugged and plopped himself down at my table. "Eat, eat!" he admonished me. "Never let the food get cold."

I found out that his name was Chris L'Esperance, that he was an artist, and that he had a collection of some 150 cherubs and angels. Which was when it hit me like a celestial brick.

"Are you an angel?" I inquired.

Chris roared with big, booming laughter. "Maybe. Are you?"

"Not that I know of. But you have all the qualifications of an angel according to my friend Terry Taylor, who's writing a book on them. You're happy and friendly and you like to laugh and you just brought me a mysterious angelic gift."

Chris looked at me intently. "Is there anything else you need?"

"Yeah," I said. "About five thousand dollars, before April 15th."

"Taxes?"

"Uh huh."

"When is April 15th?"

"Two weeks. Never mind, I know it's ridiculous. I can't think of a single way five thousand dollars is going to come into my life between now and then."

He was silent for a moment.

"You'll have the money," he pronounced presently. "Not in two weeks. But in three. You're going to have a lot of money. A lot of money."

Something about the way he said that gave me a tingly feeling.

I don't know why, but I just knew that he wasn't your average, everyday Los Angeles cornflake.

I raced home to call Terry. "I met an angel!" I babbled, as soon as she answered. "Wait till you see this cherub he sold me. And he says I'm going to have my tax money in three weeks."

Terry just laughed her wonderful, tinkly laugh. "That's great," she said. "But just remember that angels can be off by a few weeks, or even months. Time isn't one of their strong points."

"If he's off by years, what'll I tell the IRS?"

"Oh, he's probably pretty much on target. Don't worry."

Three days later, I was sitting in my agent's home when the phone rang. He excused himself and came back about five minutes later.

"How would you like a check for eight thousand dollars?" he asked.

I got that tingly feeling again.

"How?"

"That was an editor. They've got a book project, and they're looking for a writer. You'd be great."

Well, to make a long story short, I got the job and a check for over eight thousand dollars five weeks later.

"That angel was only two weeks off," I told Terry when I took her out to dinner to celebrate.

"That's not bad. They can really go out in left field sometimes. But that's usually only when they're having fun with you, like when you ask for something really stupid. This one knew you needed the money."

Anyway, there are such things as angels, and they do come into your life when you call on them, and even when you don't. And Terry Taylor will show you how to get in touch with them, how to spot them, how to utilize them, and, most importantly, how to learn to love life the way they do. Angels, you see, are not just the winged beings of Judeo-Christian heavyosity who reside within the dusty halls of biblical lore. Nor are they dead people sprouting feathers. Not in Terry's book, anyway. As she so convincingly explains, angels walk the earth just as you and I do, and in fact could very well be you and I, for each and every one of us has angel potential just waiting to be unleashed. Terry has encountered angels in the form of gas station attendants, drifters, waitresses, you name it. (I myself met an angel posing as a counter girl at one of L.A.'s most obnoxious MacDonald's.) And once you begin to be able to sniff out angels yourself, life suddenly becomes a never-ending adventure, in which those you meet are no longer faceless strangers but rather possible harbingers of joy.

Through Terry, I soon became adept at making contact with the heavenly kingdom. I learned about angel mail, a technique whereby you can send letters to the angels of various people whose aid you're seeking or whose annoyance you'd like to obliterate once and for all. I learned about angel conferences, in which you can summon as many angels as you like for a board meeting to discuss and resolve the agenda of your life. I learned about angel satchels, convenient forms of baggage that are smaller and lighter than a breadbox, in which you can place people or situations who are bothering you and let the angels take care of the air freight. Most of all, I learned how to give up the things in life that distressed me, surrendering them to the care of the cosmos, and to actually believe that I could have anything that I wanted out of life.

Well, almost anything. The angels never gave me the marriage that I thought I wanted, with the man I thought I wanted. This really bothered me. "So what's with this angel mail?" I said crossly to Terry one day, six months after I had sent a letter to my dearly beloved's highest angel asking for us to get back together. "It's been six months and I haven't heard a thing from the angels. Their postal system must be worse than Italy's."

"Just trust," Terry assured me. "If they're not getting you something, it's for a good reason."

I'll say. On a worthiness scale of one to ten, this man turned out to be a minus six. He eventually made my life so miserable that I was seriously considering joining the Jesuits. And a year after I'd used angel mail, the man I'd truly waited for all my life just happened along.

"You see?" said Terry. "You just mailed the letter to the wrong person, that's all. It took the angels a year to track down the right address."

So, I'm a convert to angelology. And after you read Terry's book, chances are you will be, too. I hope so, because once you let the angels take care of everything that once drove you crazy, you'll find yourself on the road to true happiness. So pack all your troubles in the old angel satchel and smile, smile, smile. The angels are here.

Mary Beth Crain

Preface

The purpose of this book is to expand your awareness of angels. This book is not about whether or not you believe angels exist (this is not up for debate); it is about knowing and noticing the ways of angels so you can incorporate angel help into your everyday life.

There are many popular positive-thinking and self-help books around; *Messengers of Light* is *not* another positive-thinking book. Angels are the missing link in the chain of self-help titles. These ever-helpful messengers of divine providence have thus far been neglected in the context of self-help, self-development, and self-reliance programs that expect people to do everything by and for themselves. Angels are heaven-sent agents who are always available to help you create heaven in your life. This book will help you expand and develop your awareness of angels so you can obtain unseen help with your spiritual growth and happiness.

If you listen, you will hear angels in the lyrics of songs. You may even see angels in faces, paintings, windows, or the sky. You may feel them touch you gently on the shoulder. You may find yourself reading about them in the newspaper or hearing about them on the evening news. And you may notice their jasmine or rose scent in the strangest places. Looking for angels will bring them to you.

About the Structure of This Book

Messengers of Light is divided into five parts, sequentially designed so that the information introduced in each part will be useful in the following parts.

The chapters are kept short for several reasons. For one, angels are light and playful. They do not want information about their ways to overwhelm anyone. Also, the philosophy behind this book is not to give pat answers, but to encourage you, the reader, to come up with creative questions to answer and problems to solve for yourself, in your own special way, with your own special awareness of how angels can assist you. Short chapters also enable you to skip around the book and read whatever appeals to you in the moment.

Part One covers the nature and origin of angels in a "light" manner. Angels have been around for a long time and have taken various forms in almost all of the world's religions and cultures. This section discusses angels in terms of their own realm, which is heaven.

Part Two introduces the angels you will be reading about throughout the book, and gives examples and definitions of the various "halos" angels wear. This section will explore the roles angels play and their special activities.

Part Three is the method section; in it, you will discover ways to attract the angels described in Part Two, and ways to get their attention focused on you for achieving favorable consequences and joyful living.

Part Four is about leading a more angelic life. This section gives a few ideas and practices meant to help you incorporate your higher self into your everyday life.

Part Five offers a potpourri of noteworthy angel propaganda. It includes descriptions of other people's experiences with angels, and it also lists other books and miscellaneous information on angels.

Keeping an angel journal will be helpful as you read the book, for writing down thoughts about angels and for putting into practice the methods recommended in the various chapters. See the introduction to Part Three for more on keeping an angel journal.

How I Came to Write This Book

You may wonder, before or after reading this book, where I got my information and why I decided to write a book on angels.

For as long as I can remember, I always knew that angels existed and I always thought they were a good idea. My philosophy was: Why question something that makes so much sense to me? So, instead of trying to disprove the existence of angels, I collected positive information about them and stored it in "the back of my mind" as an ongoing research project. As a teenager, I tended to be a bit reckless, and I had a friend who also had this tendency. I remember that each time we had a close call, we would comment that our guardian angels were probably fed up with working overtime. We also discovered that our guardians could do other special things besides saving us all the time. We figured out that if we asked them they would help us get things we wanted. When I look back at the silly things we asked for, I see how truly patient and loving they were with us, and that is the beauty of it. All human requests, regardless of importance, will be considered by angels and brought to pass if they are for the highest loving good for all concerned (or, at the least, if they aren't exactly harmful).

Approximately five years ago, my research project gained momentum with the help of my close friend and spiritual witness Shannon. Together, we began looking in earnest for books and various other sources on angels and their ways. We started searching out people who we thought either were angels or had had experiences with angels. Whenever we met someone, we would ask, "Have you ever seen an angel?" We started noticing and sharing the synchronistic events the angels gave us. Most of all, we discovered how fun and light life can be when angels are around in full force.

When I started out with the idea for a book about angels, initially I was going to try to attribute all mystical, metaphysical, and psychic experiences to angels. I was going to include all the extraterrestrials and channeled entities I'd been told about under the banner of angels. I was also going to try not to talk about God in the book for fear of turning off some readers. Well, when I actually started writing about angels, I was led in a different direction. I found that the experiences people had with extraterrestrials just didn't fit the experiences that I and others have had with angels. In fact, they were very different at the core.

Because these are subjective experiences and the theories about them are so elusive in nature, I won't go into the details. I will point out a major difference I found in the stories about extraterrestrials or "disembodied spirits" versus those about angels. The major difference is that in all the nonangel situations, there was a great deal of *interference* (positive and/or negative) in the life of the person who was receiving the messages or experience, and the messages came in the form of "words," often including very verbose details. In contrast, the angel experiences consisted of joyful feelings, strong intuition, inspiration, and a sense of "permissionary" noninterference. Words as such were not used by the angels; rather, the "communications" were interpreted into words only later by the person to describe what was meant and how they felt. In every case, the angel experience left the person with a sense of well-being and deep peace.

I also found it awkward to talk about angels without mentioning God. It seemed silly when I tried to think of angels flying randomly in circles — just happening to do something nice once in a while, without some sort of leader or higher being in charge, or without an ultimate purpose. So, when I do mention God in the book, I mean to represent the love that is the angels' raison d'être — the love that they play with to maintain love in the universe.

My information has come from various sources: experiences, literature, and the people I know. The main source I used for the book was my strongest intuitions regarding angels, which came from a synthesis of all the outside information I've taken in and all the inside information I have from a deep sense of knowing. And, of course, I asked the angels to inspire me at all times. I don't feel I have "channeled" angels in the traditional sense, because angels speak to us in feelings and guide us by inspiration. Most of all, angels give me the feeling that I'm not alone in the universe, and that I am loved. I have tried to remain true to myself and to the angels. I wrote this book to share information that has made my life fun, happy, meaningful, exciting, successful, loving, easy to take, and less serious!

Here are some of the main messages angels have for us: Life is really not serious, and humor and levity equal creativity. Life can be beautiful, like the colors of heaven. Humans need to incorporate celestial play and joy into their lives. We can trust the loving ways of angels and in turn learn to trust and love ourselves.

Angels make life happier and easier. Use this book as a guidebook to the realm of the angels. Discover ways to create angel awareness and to attract angels into your life. If you do, the angels will share with you their antistress, antigravity, and antiaging secrets.

Acknowledgments

Writing this book was fun. When people found out I was writing a book on angels, they all had something positive to say and often positive help to offer. The angels brought many new friends into my life in the last couple of years, and brought me closer to those I already had. There are many people I would like to thank for their help and inspiration in making this book a reality.

First of all, I would like to thank Francis Jeffrey. I told him lightly (after buying a book about angels that didn't cover the subject matter I wanted) that I was going to write a book about angels. I wasn't really serious at the time, but he convinced me that I could do it. He assisted in the writing, contributed many new ideas, and helped me clarify my own ideas. He also wrote a wonderful essay for the Angel Forum in Part Five.

After realizing that I could, should, and must write this book, I tried to bring my long-time friend and spiritual sister Shannon Boomer in on the project. She convinced me that I could write the book by myself, but that she would help. Much of this book came from experiences we have had together and from long conversations about angels over the past five years—so in many ways she did write this with me and I owe her many thanks.

Next, I would like to thank another long-time friend, Linda Hayden. Immediately after I told her about my idea for an angel book, Linda began gathering information for me. She also became my foremost cheerleader and was always there to encourage me with this project during all my human ups and downs. Linda knows the true meaning of beauty and its healing effects, so being around her meant the angels were at work with their magic. When I think of my friends Linda and Shannon, I know I am truly blessed.

When I told my family about the book, my father said ironically, "Well, we sure know you've been surrounded by angels in this house." The thing is, it's true. I am always surrounded by angels in their house. You see, my mother (Nancy) and my father (Gordon) are very much like angels and just don't know it. Their unconditional and unfaltering love has brought me through many difficult times and many changes. I would like to thank them for once again helping me through a change — writing this book. I also want to thank my sister Kathy, her husband Steve, and their children Elizabeth, Jessica, and Nicholas for providing some humor and fun for the book. I especially want to thank Elizabeth for the poem she contributed to the Angel Forum and Jessica for her funny comments on angels, which I used in various places. Thanks also to my brothers, Tim and Kevin, for their help and inspiration.

The angels brought my literary agent, Daniel Kaufman, right to my door. His enthusiasm, intelligence, and natural salesmanship were just what the angels ordered. He is a rare blend of artist and promoter, and amazing things happen around him. I want to thank him and his wife Gina, who is an example of true angelic beauty, for all their support and encouragement, and for the nourishing dinners they provided throughout this project. I also want to thank their baby daughter Anastasia for being an angel, and I am very grateful to Daniel for the piece he wrote on gratitude for the Angel Forum.

I must also thank Daniel for bringing Mary Beth Crain into my life. She became a key part of this project, acting as consultant and contributing the foreword and a piece for the Angel Forum. She brings true angelic wit and charm to everything she does, and true angelic genius when she writes and plays the piano. I wish to express my gratitude for her help and for becoming an instant and valued friend.

The first positive response I had from the publishing world came from Dan Joy, senior editor at J.P. Tarcher, Inc. Dan came over one evening and spent several hours helping me get the proposal in shape, and he had a lot to do with helping me find the right publisher. I thank him for all his valuable support.

The angels truly knew where to look when they wanted to find the right publisher. Hal and Linda Kramer are publishers with a vision to make the world a better and happier place to be. There could be no better publishers for this book, and I want to thank them for their insight and for their help along the way. Not all writers can call up their publishers directly, whenever necessary, and receive just what they need. I consider myself very blessed to know them.

Hal and Linda knew just where to find the right editor. Nancy Grimley Carleton came in at the end of the process and truly polished my work. I want to thank her for the long hours she spent making sure I said what I wanted to say. Also, I am very honored that she found the time to contribute a delightful piece for the Angel Forum. Thanks also to Uma Ergil, Hal and Linda's angelic assistant.

Other help from the publishing world came from the positive feedback I received from Steve Bucher of Lowertown Books (Minneapolis) and from Philip di Franco of Di Franco Productions. I thank them both for their time and their happy-go-lucky dispositions.

I wish to thank Laura Huxley for spending an afternoon talking with me about the book and for her helpful advice about the writing of books in general.

I also wish to thank Dr. Linda Zwingeberg Fickes for kindly allowing me to excerpt her article "Healing With Angels" for the Angel Forum.

I can't thank John C. Lilly enough for his sincere interest in this book and for providing a heavenly office as my workplace. His humor and mystical awareness were very inspiring and gave me many new ways to look at myself.

I owe many thanks to my friends: to Violet and Derek Budgell for their cheerleading and the wonderful angel gifts they gave me for inspiration (and to Violet for being the essence of charm); to Deirdre Briggs for her supportive and generous nature and for bringing me books and information on angels; to Laura and Dean Larson for their encouragement, for the angel theme Christmas party, and for promoting angelic beauty through Laura's art and Dean's photography; and to Diane Piazzi for fourteen years of humor, laughter, and friendship.

The community of people I lived with while writing this book provided helpful encouragement, and never a dull moment. I would like to thank Lisa Lyon-Lilly, Barbara Clarke-Lilly, Nina Lilly, Charles Lilly, Frankie Lee Slater, Rudy Vogt, and Chicharra, for always being there with encouragement, humor, excitement, and friendship.

Other friends who helped in important ways were George and Jackie Koopman, Jai Italiander, Jeannie St. Peter, Brummbaer, Larry Raithaus, Joe D. Goldstrich, Michael Siegel, Michael Shields, Patricia Le Dell, and Leticia Boyle. Thank you to Theo Katana for his love, prayers, and lessons in survival, and to his family, especially his mother and *the magic shoes.* Thank you to Kathy Faulstich for letting me overhear her angel story, and to her mother, Katherine Portland, for a lifetime of encouragement and inspiration.

Special thanks to all who participated in the angel forum whom I haven't yet mentioned: Suzanna Soloman, Thomas LeRose, Kutira Decosterd and Moonjay, Karin Jensen, Filomena, and Gideon Boomer. And also to the mysterious "K," who goes about in her cloud of angels.

I would like to thank Wesley Van Linda of Narada Productions and Kathy Tyler of InnerLinks for help with the section on their ANGEL® cards.

And I thank all the angels I've ever known.

Part One

The Nature and
Origin of Angels

Chapter 1

Angels Now
and Historically

Most of us have seen paintings of angels who look like beautiful humans with wings and flowing attire. Angels are usually depicted with halos, auras of white light that encircle their heads. When we read about angels, they are usually described in the same way, but sometimes they are said to appear as dazzling, almost blinding, white light.

How did artists and ancient scribes come to the conclusion that angels have wings and halos? Early books of the Old Testament did not depict angels this way; they were described as ordinary humans dressed in white goatskins (symbolizing purity, light, and holiness), or as wingless youths. Wings and halos showed up in Christian art around the time of the Roman emperor Constantine (A.D. 312), who converted from Roman paganism to Christianity after seeing a cross in the sky before a major battle. Before that, the Greek pantheon included winged gods such as Hermes and Eros, who, in addition to their other functions, carried messages between the gods of Olympus and the lesser gods of earth. The word *angel* comes from the Greek word *angelos*, meaning messenger. Because angels functioned as God's messengers, eventually they were thought of as having wings, like the winged gods Hermes and Eros. Wings symbolize the quickness with which angels travel carrying God's messages. The halo or aura of white light symbolizes their origin or home, which is heaven.

The pictorial image of wings and halos provided believers with a focus and an icon to adore. Soon, art was thriving with winged angels, and poetry and drama followed suit.

So, historically, angels were thought of as messengers between God and humanity. Messages we receive from God through angels are meant to bring us closer to achieving heaven on earth. As a species, we haven't really changed that much. For most of us, picturing angels with wings and halos is still the easiest way to visualize them. This is fine, because angels can appear in any form our imagination will accept.

Angels in one form or another exist in almost all of the world's great religions. They are mentioned in recorded history as far back as three thousand years before Christ. Because this book is about the present, about how angels can help us right *now*, I am not going to involve you in a detailed history of ideas about angels. Entire books have been written on this subject. I will mention just a few highlights of this story.

The ancient cultures of Egypt, Babylon, Persia, and India all acknowledged winged angels (sometimes called "gods"); it is likely that these traditions influenced the Greeks and Romans, who began painting wings on angels in the West. The Yoga Sutras of Patanjali, an Indian meditation teacher roughly contemporary with Plato, told how one could contact "celestial beings" by meditating on the light inside one's own head; these beings of light make the connection between the human and the divine realms. (I know a meditation devotee who is continuously in touch with the angelic realm, and she is enwraped in a cloud of angels wherever she goes.)

An especially significant development in angel history came from Persia, where Zoroaster (also known as Zarathushtra, ca. 628–551 B.C.) wrote in great detail in his Avesta about his encounters with a number of angels, and said that angels are extensions and projections of God toward humanity—not separate beings standing between God and humanity. (God is portrayed by Zarathushtra as presiding over a court of angels—oversized humanlike figures, both male and female, who reflect God's radiance.)

The idea that angels are expressions or extensions of God, rather than independent beings, was emphasized by the Gnostics, contemporaries of Jesus, who warned against accepting angels as intermediaries between humans and God—in effect, as "God's brokers."

There seems to be renewed interest these days in the three orders of angels with three choirs in each: The highest order consists of seraphim, cherubim, and thrones; the second order consists of dominions, virtues, and powers; and the third consists of principalities, archangels, and angels. Again, a number of books and essays interpret these concepts, and I will list some of these in the Annotated Bibliography in Part Five. The orders of angels are worth reading about if you are highly interested in how angels have participated in history and in the philosophical viewpoints concerning their existence.

Angels today are not really different from angels when they were first discovered. Angels have always been thought of as the main connection for humans between heaven and earth; although the concepts of God and heaven have varied, angels have consistently helped humans with our spiritual growth and happiness.

Chapter 2

What on Earth Is an Angel?

Close your eyes and see what comes to mind when you think of angels. Do you see a picture of any specific person? Does a specific incident come to mind? Do you experience a feeling of warmth and lightness passing over you as you imagine angels? Now, think about heaven. What colors do you see? Do you imagine beauty, peace, joy, and happiness? Do you think of heaven as a realm different from the one we live in here on earth?

There are many ways to interpret heaven, and many ways to interpret who and what angels are. The many interpretations come from the fact that we are all unique beings with unique experiences of life. To establish some common ground for the sake of this book, let us consider heaven as a realm or plane separate from the realm we live in on earth. Heaven is the realm of joy, lightness, happiness, unconditional love, laughter, and beauty. Let us consider that angels exist in heaven as separate beings of the highest divine power in the universe. They are beings of light who send information and loving thoughts through our higher self to inspire and guide us. These angelic beings have all the properties of light—speed, brightness, and the power to heal and to obliterate darkness.

Because we are unique beings, the way we experience and picture angels will vary accordingly. The angels discussed in this book simply want the highest good for all concerned, so you may picture them however you like. These angels want to help you connect your highest self with heaven, so you can be happier here on earth. Angels sense that the natural state of life is one of joy, happiness, laughter, and beauty, the qualities of heaven, the angels' own realm.

An angel is a guardian and messenger from heaven. Heaven is where miracles originate, where love exists as pure, unconditional healing energy, and where humans are regarded as a protected species having free will. An angel can bring the heaven realm to humans on earth if we want it and are willing to accept it. This book describes the various ways angels can inspire us to be happier and more creative beings—without taking away our free will. Angels do not control us, and they do not learn our lessons for us. They do, however, know our inner nature and can step in and protect us when they know we truly want it. They also have the ability to inspire us and send us messages that help us with our everyday life.

One way to think of angels is as coaches in the game of life. Coaches don't themselves play the game they are coaching, but they are still very important to the players. Coaches don't necessarily have to be able to play the game well; they just need to understand human nature. An angel can be our private coach by reminding us to include fun and happiness in our life game. Angels can coach us in bringing love, beauty, and peace into our lives. Angels cannot understand why more humans don't join in the divine cosmic dance of the universe. Angels and children get along well, because children can readily play and have fun— and they do it with joy, singing, screaming, and laughing. Angel coaches teach fun and merriment.

Most people do not take angels seriously. This is fine with

the angels, because they are free from the seriousness of our realm. They see most humans as being consumed with seriousness. Angels teach us that nothing is truly serious. We human beings can perform feats of amazing creativity when our minds are freed of the weight of seriousness. We can heal ourselves from disease (mental and physical), and we can turn our lives around by changing the way we think. Angels recognize the great number of higher possibilities with which human beings are blessed. They are assigned to teach humans the way of lightness, so that "human potential" can become "human reality."

Being human is something angels envy at times. Angels admire the human ability to enter deeply into the passion of love— to have strong convictions from the heart. They envy our freedom of choice, or free will. Free will gives us humans tremendous creative power. We have the power to create timeless gifts of art, literature, music, and great thinking to inspire the human race, even long after we are gone.

We have been given freedom of choice, meaning we can choose any spiritual or nonspiritual path we desire. Our free will gives us those little "ups and downs" we experience along the path we have chosen. Human beings are influenced by many cycles, including our natural biorhythms, the seasons of the year, energy waves, astrological movements, and so forth. It is natural to have some days that are good and some that are not so good. Our choices can help shift the low-energy days in a lighter, more energetic direction. Since we have free will, we can choose to transform or transcend the low points in our lives. At the least, we can understand that some low points are a natural part of life, and we can learn not to be distraught by them.

Sanaya Roman explains, "You choose the range of intensity of your emotions. Some of you have chosen a very broad range, from immense pain to great joy. Some of you have chosen narrower ranges, preferring to work with subtle levels, such as moderate joy to moderate unhappiness. Because you live in a polarity, for each positive emotion you have you will also have its opposite.

Emotional calm comes from finding the balance point, bringing all your emotions into harmony with your Higher Self." Angels want to teach us emotional balance, so that we can have the peak experiences of freedom and joy on their credit and not have to pay with the low opposite of human despair.

Angels work (play) behind the scenes to inspire in humans our inborn gifts of talent and genius. They also work (play) around the clock in their timeless dimension to synchronize human life. Their main function is to keep you from feeling unimportant in this vast sea of humanity. In the heavenly scheme of life, you have a special position; the angels around you are in charge of the research and development concerning your spiritual quests on the road to unconditional happiness (truly the road less traveled).

Chapter 3

Angels and Our Physical Senses

Most of us do not see angels as physical objects. Some have seen angels as fields of dazzling light, too bright to stare at for long. If you do see an angel, the angel will probably take the form you are most willing to accept. Most of us have seen pictures of angels with wings and halos. If you want to imagine angels as beautiful humans with wings, this is fine; if an angel is destined to appear to you, he or she will probably oblige you by taking such a form. Angels have appeared to people throughout history, but this is rare and generally surrounds a "big event."

To get to know angels, it helps if you can transcend the "seeing is believing" paradigm and adopt an open mind and a stance of "knowing by intuition." Reality is much more than just what we see. And it is much more than what we hear. Consider for a moment the field of electromagnetic energy that surrounds us; we know this field exists, but we cannot see or hear it with our usual physical senses. We need some kind of receiver. For example, radio and television signals are silent and invisible to us until we turn on a radio or a television set, but these signals exist around us all the time. We see physical objects through their reflection of a narrow band of the frequencies called "visible light," but we see only the rays of light that actually enter the pupils of our eyes, not the entire three-dimensional field of electromagnetic "light" energy that surrounds us.

Candace Pert is one of the scientists who discovered endorphins. Endorphins are natural opiates found in our brains that act as filtering mechanisms. Endorphins are used to filter selectively the incoming information from every sense (sight, hearing, smell, taste, touch, and pain), blocking some of it from percolating up to higher levels of consciousness. Candace Pert states, "Each organism has evolved so as to be able to detect the electromagnetic energy that will be most useful for its survival. Each has its own *window on reality*." Aldous Huxley spoke of the nervous system and the brain being a "reducing valve," or filter, that enables us to experience only a fraction of reality.

If environmental information is filtered selectively by every sense, and if there are happenings around us that are not registered in our usual waking consciousness, then consider this: Part of the reality that we filter out is angelic activity. Angels are very busy, and they exist in many places at once; if we could see them readily, we would experience chaos, and we might all go crazy. When saints and mystics hear voices and see visions, other people get frightened and tend to label them "insane."

Legend has it that in ancient times angels, fairies, elves, brownies, and various other magical creatures were easy to see and talk to (perhaps this is the origin of folklore and fairy tales). Anyway, humans became so preoccupied with the magic of this realm that they were not paying attention to the physical world. So for growth and survival reasons humans for the most part had to "turn off" the ability to see and hear these magical creatures. I have talked to several people who do "see" angels, but they don't like to talk or boast about it, because it is very personal to them and of a sacred nature.

When we "hear" angels, we may hear a beautiful chorus of voices singing in the distance. I have heard about cases of angels embellishing the music a person is listening to with their singing (if they like it). Or you may "hear" sweet tingling bells or chimes at subtle times when angels are around you.

Angels sometimes leave a fragrant scent around for us to smell, in places where we can't figure out where the scent is coming from. Two floral scents they especially like are rose and jasmine.

Some people know angels are with them because at strategic times they feel a hand touch gently upon their shoulder or feel a presence so strong and calming it compels them to look around for someone who isn't there.

Don't worry if you are not able to have magical, imagistic, or physical sensations regarding angels. Angels are not here to interfere with our growth, and some of us get carried away with magical thinking and mystical experiences. The most important attitude to cultivate in attracting angels is one of optimistic, unconditional love and happiness. Angels surround the truly happy and loving person, encouraging more love and happiness. Whether you can experience them readily with your physical senses is unimportant. What matters is finding a way to know angels for yourself, and steering clear of the "seeing is believing" nonsense we have all heard at one time or another.

Angels are like thoughts. We cannot see our thoughts, but we know they exist. We can have as many thoughts as we want; there is no limit. Imagine for a moment a source field where thoughts become form. Think of a positive loving thought as a blessing. Imagine how it travels as a healing beam of light to whomever the thought was about. See it reach the person and lighten up his/her heart and mind. Now that person has a light heart and sends out blessings to those around. The original blessing has created a chain reaction of happiness that reaches out to more and more people. Now imagine what a negative thought can do. I won't describe each link in this chain, but I'm sure your imagination will help you see the damage negative thoughts can do.

Thoughts are powerful and real even though we don't see them—and so are angels. All of us have our "own window on reality," so we experience angels in our own way. There is, however, a common denominator: Angels don't hurt us; they help us. Any messages, experiences, happening, thoughts, and feelings that interfere with or limit our well-being and separate us further from our highest self do not originate from angels. Angels exist in a realm of positive, loving energy and pink love light. When we have peak experiences of joy and love, we have connected with the angels. Angels don't *have* peak experiences; they *are* peak experiences. (Angels don't experience the ups and downs we humans do.) Angels serve as models of the joyful and happy thoughts that we can share.

Chapter 4

God as the Origin of Angels

To know and understand the ways of angels, you must realize that God is their boss. Angels work for God in various capacities to maintain the loving order of the universe. God is the origin, and angels are God's first creation. Don't let the word "God" scare you or turn you off. If necessary, whenever you see God mentioned in this book, substitute a term that makes you feel more comfortable, such as "the Universe," "Mother Nature," "the Great Spirit," or whatever name puts you in touch with a higher power. Just keep in mind that angels belong to a loving higher order, which they work and play to maintain. Also, please keep in mind that God and the angels have an outrageous sense of humor.

The bottom line is that God is love, and that we are loved unconditionally by God. We are always free; God does not love us because of what we do or how much *we* love God. God loves us up-front, and whenever we want this love it is consistently available. Because there are no fixed guidelines or rules to follow for receiving unconditional love, we sometimes become perplexed and want to know how we're doing. We humans are always looking for signs of approval or disapproval. We want clear boundaries to tell us how far we can go and what line we cannot cross over. We seem to want uniforms to wear, rules to follow, and outlines of our fate and destiny to fulfill.

There are no rules or formulas for finding good favor and love from God. God's love *has* to be unconditional because God gave us free will. If we didn't have free will, we would probably be sent to earth with a set of instructions and rules describing what we are supposed to do in this lifetime, and what our main purpose is supposed to be. But because we have free will we can step over any boundary, break any rule, and take off any uniforms. So where does that leave us? Loved and basically free. Our freedom is what makes us truly great, but it can also get us into trouble and cause us to miss joyful opportunities.

Some human beings spend their whole lives trying to figure out what kinds of actions will please God. They can't stand the idea that it is so easy, that God loves us no matter what we do. God loves us even when we don't love ourselves. God's message is love and forgiveness—to love and forgive ourselves, and to treat ourselves kindly.

Why are we even here? I certainly can't answer that question for you. Maybe life is all a big joke and we are let in on the punch line when we die and then spend eternity laughing hysterically. One thing I do know is that if we use our free will to make ourselves happy life is much easier, much more creative, and much more humorous. In short, it is much more fun. Free will accounts for the ups and downs of life. The ups and downs are just part of the game; ideally, the downs will help you appreciate and take advantage of the ups. Because angels don't have ups and downs in their realm, they can help bring you up faster when you've gotten down.

El Shaddai is a name for God that means "the God who is more than enough," the God who is much more than we could even desire. God wants us to be happy, and angels are God's emissaries to help us create happiness on earth. If we can learn ways to trust the abundance of a God who is more than enough, then we will have more than enough, even enough to give away, which will bring us even more.

This talk about God is *not* meant to offer you yet another belief system or cosmology; it is meant to let you know that angels come from the realm of heaven, where a pure source of unconditional love (which I have called God) exists for all of us. Unconditional love is our source of healing, happiness, and bliss; it is the ultimate freedom. Angels want us to find pure unconditional love for ourselves — to find God in ourselves — so that we will be free to create our lives as gifts that continue to give throughout time.

Don Gilmore, author of *Angels, Angels, Everywhere,* defines angels as "forms, images, or expressions through which the essences and energy forces of God can be transmitted. An Angel is a form through which a specific essence or energy force can be transmitted for a *specific purpose.*" In Part Two of this book, you will learn about angels in terms of the various spiritual essences and energy forces of God they adopt. I use the term "halo" to represent the various forms and images angels transmit from God for specific purposes in our lives.

Part Two

Halos
Angels Wear

About Part Two:

Classifications of Angels

Angels of divine providence act in a variety of ways. Part Two will expose you to the busy angelic realm. You will learn about the many "halos" (or "hats") angels wear, which denote the specific essence, energy force, or spiritual expression they represent from God and heaven. A halo is a band of light that encircles an angel's head; this circle of light constantly connects the angel with heaven. Halos also provide a system of classification. In Part Two, I will describe angels in terms of certain classifications symbolized by their halos. Each chapter (big halo) has several subsections (small halos) that describe more specialized classifications of angel vocations.

Chapter 5 in Part Two is about our personal angels, who are integrated with our higher self. These angels stay around us all the time to inspire, guide, and protect. Our personal angels watch over the many spiritual paths available to us, and they act as guides and teachers to accelerate our spiritual growth. They stay nearby, cheering us on and awakening our creativity to its highest potential. Angels are always in close contact with our higher self. The higher self exists in a realm separate from our physical reality. In this realm, the higher self can remain in continuous contact with angels (if we want this and are open to it). This is why it is sometimes so effective to communicate by asking our guardian angel to speak to the guardian angel of someone else concerning our deepest and highest desires.

Chapter 6 is about angels of the moment. Angels of the moment come to us at those times when we need extra help. They help heal us when we are sick; they rescue us when we are lost, in trouble, or in danger; they provide coincidental events that remind us of the divine providence and order in the universe; they transform grave situations so that seriousness leaves and humor prevails; and they sometimes engineer miracles.

Chapter 7 introduces angels who embellish human life. These angels "make life worth living," so to speak. They provide us with unconditional happiness, fun, and mirth. They also help out with romance and wealth. And they help us extinguish worries that plague our lives.

Chapter 8 concerns angel psychologists. Angel psychologists help us understand and analyze ourselves by acting as brain program editors. Wearing this professional halo, they bring an awareness of internal behavior patterns, so that we can take advantage of the freedom to change our behavior if we so desire. Angels help us become the best we can be. Angels are also the beings behind the mythological gods and goddesses of ancient Greece, Rome, and India. These archetypal angels help us understand ourselves because they represent the original models for human personality.

Nature has en entire hierarchy of angels collectively known as the devic kingdom. Chapter 9 gives a quick overview of this devic kingdom, of the angels and lesser beings who are in charge of flora and fauna.

Chapter 10 tells you how to design your own flock of angels. You can name these angels and call upon them for help with any situation that arises. This will prove helpful if you need angelic assistance for a specific area in your life that is not included in the angels' job descriptions elsewhere in Part Two.

Remember, angels are like thoughts; you can have as many as you want for help and guidance. After reading Part Two, think about how angels work in your life. Then, read Part Three to learn how you can employ as many angels as you want using the methods for attracting angels into your life.

Chapter 5

Personal Angels

Guardian Angels

*For He will give His Angels [especial] charge concerning you,
To guard you in all your ways.*

                                        Psalms 91:11

A guardian angel is assigned to each person on earth. Each
human being, regardless of belief, status, shape, or size has
the privilege of a guardian angel. Your guardian angel is with
you all the time, wherever you go, whatever you do. It has been
said that when God looks at you God sees two—you and your
guardian angel. When French farmers traveled a road alone
and would meet up with another single traveler, they would
greet one another by saying, "Good day to you and your companion" ("companion" meaning "guardian angel"). Your guardian angel has been with you throughout time and was there
when you decided to come into this world as the special human you are today. Your guardian angel remembers and keeps
track of the high goals you set for yourself, the high aspirations

21

you have stored deep in your unconscious mind.

My first memory of my guardian angel goes back to when I was three years old. I was playing in an off-limits area in our backyard with one of my teddy bears. Somehow, the teddy bear fell down a ravine. I stood looking at it for a minute, trying to decide whether to forget it or go and get it. I decided to go and get it, because it was the smallest bear in my collection and therefore important. I took one step toward the ravine and heard a voice say, "No, don't go down there; leave the teddy bear and go back up to the house." I remember feeling as if there were a barrier between me and the ravine. Considering that I wasn't supposed to be there in the first place, I left and went back up to the house with only the memory of my teddy bear. I remember thinking that he would make friends with some little animals and everything would be okay.

You may remember a time in your life when you were reckless and could have been seriously hurt, and it seemed like an invisible force pulled you to safety. Maybe you don't have a story like this but have heard one or read one somewhere. Guardian angels are known to most of us who drive cars, especially on the freeway. Many times, I've experienced that cars that were heading for an accident with me were lifted or pushed out of the way at just the right moment to avoid a collision.

When people sustain serious physical injuries and someone comes at just the right time to save their lives, the rescuer usually came because something told him or her to get there quick. The injured person's guardian angel went to the other person's guardian angel and relayed the emergency message. Basically, guardian angels are known for protecting and guarding us in all our activities on earth.

Why not explore ways to get to know your personal guardian angel? There are many ways your guardian angel can help you, beyond saving you from car accidents and bodily harm. Develop an intimate relationship with your guardian angel. You can ask your guardian angel for knowledge and insight about confusing situations in your life. You can also ask him or her to speak to the guardian angels of any people in your life concerning the involvements you have with them. Pay attention to your intuition; it will become more brilliant when you are in harmony with your guardian angel, for it is through the inner knowing of intuition that you will receive messages from your guardian angel to warn and guide you. Have you ever stopped yourself from doing something because you suddenly had a strong sense it would be a mistake, only to find out later that, if you had followed through, it would have been disastrous?

Be creative with your guardian angel. In private, be like a child who has an invisible friend and confidant — guardian angels enjoy this. Children have been known to see and talk to their guardian angels. This usually happens before children can communicate exactly what they see, but some of us can remember far enough back in our lives to a time when we spoke with and saw our guardian angels. If you have children, study their behavior when they are alone. Many children have invisible friends they talk to wherever they are, and babies sometimes seem to stare at someone who isn't there. When babies giggle and grin while sleeping, some say that they are playing with the angels. It is also fun to ask children what they think angels are and to have them draw an angel.

In Catholic grade school, children are taught about their guardian angels in first grade. They are taught that their guardian angels are faithful friends who help them while they are on earth by giving them messages of what God wants them to do, and who guard them from evil. Teachers may even encourage the children to move over in their seats to make room for their guardian angels. The Guardian Angel Prayer (see the end of this section) is recited each day. A friend of mine who is in her sixties remembers her teacher telling the children in her class that if they didn't finish their rosary prayers for some reason they didn't need to worry because their guardian angels would finish it for them.

At certain times in children's development, their guardian
angels call in assistants. Extra help is usually needed during the
"terrible twos," when children need to explore their boundaries.
After things have settled down (depending on the child), extra
help is usually not needed until a child becomes a teenager and
starts driving. At this point, some teenagers could use an army
of guardian angels, but suffice it to say that most teenagers have
at least two guardian angels working overtime to protect them
during this generally reckless period. Help may not be needed
as much during the twenties, when people learn that they are
not indestructible. Later in life, extra help will vary according
to need.

Many human beings suffer through life, and they may regress
in their evolution because they are deeply unhappy about something. Unconsciously, they seem to be trying to kill themselves
with the choices they make and the way they react to life. Unhappy humans are frustrating to the guardian angels who watch
over them. Angels are certainly not going to participate in unhappiness, so there is nothing for them to do except wait for that
one instant when the person chooses to stop suffering and a
transformation can take place. We have free will, so if we want
to suffer, or if we think that is what we are supposed to do, it
is our choice.

Sometimes it seems that our guardian angels have taken a vacation. Something awful happens that we cannot believe God or
our guardian angel would allow. One of the great mysteries of
life is why bad things happen to good people, and why good
things happen to bad people. We can speculate and come up
with explanations such as karma, lessons we must learn, and so
forth, but some of the injustice that happens on this earth can
never be explained satisfactorily. Our guardian angels never really
go on vacation, but the more positive and "optimystic" we are the
easier we are to protect and nurture. So fill the moment with
the trust, hope, and faith that your guardian angel will always
take care of you. Don't worry about tomorrow or about the

misfortune of others. Be grateful you are who you are right now, and give thanks to your guardian angel.

Always keep in mind that you have a guardian angel, who is the same today, yesterday, and tomorrow. Your guardian angel wants to remind you that at this very moment you are alive, and that whether or not you are happy about this fact it is true. Your biological and mental "machine" is running on some level of efficiency, and your guardian angel wants to keep you from feeling like a victim. Your guardian angel is looking out for you, waiting for your next step; whether it is from misery to normalcy, from normalcy to feeling good, or from feeling good to total happiness and delight, your guardian angel wants to guide you toward the next higher step. Your guardian angel is always by your side, to remind you of the important and special part you play on this crowded planet.

Reciting the Guardian Angel Prayer from the Catholic tradition can help you focus on your guardian angel's presence.

Angel of God, my guardian dear,
To whom His love commits me here;
Ever this day [or night], be at my side,
To light and guard, to rule and guide.

Messengers

The New Testament was first written in Greek, and the word for angel comes from the Greek word for messenger, *angelos.* The Old Testament was first written in Hebrew, and the Hebrew word for angel is *malakh,* which also means messenger. In both the New and Old Testaments, there are many stories of angels appearing to humans with messages. These messages usually concerned major events, for example, announcing the birth of the messiah. We don't hear of angels appearing that much anymore, but they are still relaying messages to us. Because we don't always see and hear them physically, we have to be especially creative and perceptive to receive our messages.

Angels have ways of relaying messages we don't expect. Have you ever found yourself sitting for hours at a desk racking your brain for the answer to a question or problem? Just as you've decided to stop your pondering, a dove flies onto your windowsill. Noticing this dove gives you a sense of warmth and peace, and you find yourself walking toward the window. Then, as you look out the window, a truck goes by with words written on it that give you the answer you spent so much time trying to force out of your brain. As soon as you were able to release the struggle the message came to you effortlessly.

Pay attention to the subtleties in life. Angels have many ways of reaching you, but often you miss them. For example, a child, in a moment of spontaneity, may blurt out a statement for which only you know the meaning. While thumbing through a book, a page may fall open with a clear message in the print. Headlines in the newspaper, taken out of context, might contain your message. Angels with messages often appear to us in dreams. Angels are very creative in the ways they communicate with us; we have to be just as creative when we listen for our messages.

Messages from heaven are always for the highest good of all concerned. If you receive messages or impressions that *seem* positive, but don't *feel* positive, ask yourself, "Does this message resonate with unconditional love?" Usually, a very clear yes or no answer will come to you. Messages from heaven never urge force or domination in situations, and they are usually (but not always) general rather than specific. Detailed instructions, such as "Walk to the corner, buy some cigarettes, smoke one, then call your neighbor and tell him off," are clearly not messages from heaven. Heavenly messages are often along the lines of "Don't worry. . . . Be creative. . . . Everything is all right. . . . All is well. . . . Trust. . . . "

Angels inspire us through mystical insight and sudden brilliant, or even bizarre, ideas. Some of us experience angels as inner spiritual forces that guide the higher self by instilling noble thoughts and ideals into our consciousness. All angels are messengers of some sort, regardless of the specific roles they play. Angels who are couriers of God have important news to carry. These messengers will keep at you until you receive their news, so remember to relax, release, and let your intuition guide you.

Spiritual Guides

When the pupil is ready, the teacher appears.

Spiritual guides come in and out of our lives according to need. They usually represent the essence of a particular culture, race, or religion, or they can represent a career or avenue of life. They are teachers.

When a new guide comes to you, you may find yourself with a voracious urge to know all there is to know about a particular culture or religion previously foreign to you. You start buying books, artifacts, incense, music, or clothes that will teach you the essence of this new interest and its spiritual offerings. Soon, people come into your life who are also studying the same essence in their own spiritual quests. Whether this process happens suddenly or subtly, it offers an opportunity for growth in a new direction.

Through meditation or other means, you may be able to see your guides. Basically, all you need to do is notice where your interests lie and listen to messages from within. When you discover your guide or guides, you can accelerate the pace of the lessons you are learning, as you explore the many possibilities for growth and for guidance.

For example, if one of your spiritual guides is a Native American, you may have visions that put you in touch with Mother Earth, which may bring you greater respect for the planet, which in turn may drive you to take action in some way.

If your guide is a Zen Buddhist, your lesson may concern losing your ego for a while, developing intuition, and learning to be. You may even change jobs to something more basic and less mental in order to learn new ways of being.

It may be that one of your guides represents a personality from the past, such as Florence Nightingale. In this case, your guide may portend a time of service and attention to health and nourishment.

If your guide is Celtic, you may find yourself fascinated with fairy faiths, Arthurian legends, kings and queens, harps, and mystics.

Spiritual guides teach us about spiritual values that are unfamiliar to us. Recognizing our guides through the subtle or dramatic shifts we make in our lives will help us understand our inner goals or a particular spiritual quest. Our guides never really leave us, but they may fade so that other guides can come to us when there are new lessons to learn. Spiritual guides are angels of basic teachings; they give us new insight and new creativity to bring us into harmony with our higher self.

Muses

Creativity comes from the spiritual realm, the collective consciousness. And the mind is in a different realm than the molecules of the brain. The brain is a receiver, not a source.

                                                        Candace Pert

Muses are creativity ministers who inspire our talents and gifts. We are all capable of creativity of some kind, but often we need to understand that the wellspring of creativity may rest in a world we don't see. Regardless of where our talents lie, there are muses ready to inspire us far beyond the limits we place on our humanness. There are no limits to creativity when we are inspired by angels. Creativity goes beyond talent to genius when humans develop their ability to listen to inspiration.

In Greek mythology, there are nine muses, the daughters of Mnemosyne (Memory), who were part of Apollo's retinue. These nine daughters were the goddesses of inspiration: Clio of history, Melpomene of tragedy, Urania of astronomy, Thalia of comedy, Terpsichore of dance, Calliope of epic poetry, Erato of love verse, Euterpe of lyric poems or music, and Polyhymnia of sacred or religious music.

You may notice that there are three muses directly representing poetry, and many past and contemporary poets acknowledge muses as the source of their inspiration. William Blake, an angel artist and poet once said, "I am not ashamed, to tell you what ought to be told—that I am under the direction of messengers from heaven, daily and nightly." Blake attributed all artistic genius to angels.

In Rome, it was customary to thank the genius of the house—the *lares*—at every meal; some homes even set a place for this angel. The *lares* was the spirit of the family's founder and the source of the family's creativity; genius was a part of everyday life. The word *genius* comes from the name for an ancient Roman male's guardian spirit. Juno is the name for the female's guardian spirit. At ancient birthday celebrations, the Romans honored the genius spirits, recognizing them as the source of the individual's imagination.

To muse means to meditate and reflect for creative inspiration. Whenever you need creative insight, muse away. Get in touch with your own creativity ministers, special angels who can speak to you with inspiration for your particular talent in this lifetime. Whether your gift is solving mathematical problems, painting a masterpiece, or composing great music and literature, learn to listen to your inner guidance to transform talent into genius. Please note that the existence of creative muses does not mean that we can't take credit for our artistic and creative achievements. We are the ones clever enough to expand our consciousness to allow their input, and we are the ones who do the actual work. So give yourself credit for being the genius you are.

Cheerleaders

Several years ago, I found myself wanting to make a major change in my life. While I knew this change would make my life happier, I wasn't sure how the people closest to me would react. I knew that many of them would not support my decision. My decision was leading to painful feelings of guilt, until I discovered my personal cheering section.

Coming out of a meditative state, I got the image of tiny cheerleaders cheering my life on, no matter what I chose to do, even if it was a choice no one else supported. These cheerleaders were cheering, "We like who you are" and "You deserve to be happy; go for it." I then had the courage to go ahead with my deepest desire, and in time everything worked out for the highest good of all concerned.

You, too, have an angelic cheering section for your higher self. These angels cheer with little voices, "Don't give up. . . . We like who you are. . . . Everything's going to be okay. . . . We are proud of you." There are some angels who cheer almost everything you do. Their main purpose and function is to support your decisions unconditionally without advice. This is nice when you want to make an eccentric or drastic change and other people seem to be holding you back.

Of course, you won't hear your cheerleaders' voices if you are about to do something unkind or destructive. Below the levels of goodness, the cheerleaders are silent.

Quite often, our deepest desires are difficult to follow because we judge ourselves and our position too harshly. We listen to the advice of others, instead of to our inner self. To know and follow our deepest aspirations will bring us luck. Sometimes, this may require taking a risk or two, so, if you venture out on the road of your convictions and find yourself feeling alone, remember that your cheering section and your guardian angel are there with you and that loneliness is only temporary. Listen closely; your cheering section is sending words of encouragement: "Go, team, go! Take the ball and run. . . . Don't look back!"

Copilots

As copilots, angels fly second in command on your life voyage. If you ever need them to take over, they are ready and capable. In fact, if you become disorganized, it is a good idea to let your copilot fly for a while. The pieces of your life that are scattered all around will fall into order, and you can relax and get some rest or play while you are guided back on track.

Copilots act as your invisible secretaries, arranging and ordering your days so that you don't have to make extra trips, reminding you about appointments and deadlines you are about to miss in your confusion. Take advantage of your personal secretary and give out some dictation. Dictate what time you want to get up in the morning, and how you want your days to pass. (See Chapter 20 in Part Three on the bedtime angel review.) Be specific, set deadlines, and ask your copilot to clear out confusion. Be creative and personal with your copilot angel and find new ways to accomplish your tasks so that you'll have plenty of time to create an enjoyable life.

Soul Angels

Many people ask, "Do we become angels when we die, so that we can watch over those we love?" There is a wide range of answers in the various books that address the subject of death and "near-death experiences." Some support this theory, and others don't. Some say that angels are beings created completely separate from humans.

Some people who have had a near-death experience, or who have done a guided imagery exercise of their own death, say that when they left their body deceased relatives and loved ones were there as angels to guide them into the other realm. A lot of the angel books I've read relate stories about deceased loved ones relaying important messages back to earth. These stories are very detailed and interesting and the messages usually save a life or something similarly dramatic.

According to one Tibetan Buddhist idea, each of us is a composite of aspects drawn from bygone and living personages who have influenced us in some way. Upon death, the composite disassembles and is distributed into the universe, especially to loved ones and those we have influenced. This process would leave the spirit free of its humanness in the other realm, and would benefit humans left behind. If you have loved ones who have died, remember this idea and claim a part of their composite that you could use in your own life. If you are drawn to a personality from the past, say, for example, to Thomas Jefferson, decide what it is that attracts you and take this facet into you to embellish your own composite.

Because there are so many theories concerning this subject, I will leave it to you to decide. Whatever else you do, take the love you have deep in your soul for the loved one who has crossed over and ask that this love continue to grow and transform, ask that this love watch over you. Every once in a while, I feel a blast of love coming to me from someone I have loved who has died. This is a very special feeling and is very close to the feelings I receive from my contact with angels, and very often this feeling gives me insight and inspiration. Unconditional love has no limits; it can pass back and forth through time and space in an instant. Allow yourself to experience this process directly.

Chapter 6

Angels of the Moment

Healers

There is more than enough evidence to support the theory that what goes on in our minds profoundly affects what goes on in our bodies. Healing the body can begin with healing the mind, supplying the mind with what it needs to be healthy and happy. Eliminating negative beliefs that detract from health and replacing them with positive healing thoughts also helps the body heal. (See Chapter 8 on brain program editors.) Today, many people are healing themselves by changing the way they think, by changing their attitude toward themselves and toward life.

It is interesting to note the *Oxford American Dictionary*'s definition of "to heal." These are some of the phrases used: to make whole or sound; to bring to an end or conclusion conflicts between people and groups; to settle and reconcile; to free from evil, cleanse and purify; to form healthy flesh again—to unite after being cut or broken. So, in essence, healing involves repairing and making whole after a separation or break in one's life. Healing is the act of cleaning up messes left over from the past.

Angels can serve as healing agents in many ways. They can help us heal ourselves by channeling healing rays from God. They can help us settle our conflicts with other humans. They can relay messages of forgiveness and reconciliation to others in our lives if we are willing to forgive and forget. Even if the people in question are no longer alive, angels can reach them.

You can ask healing angels for insight into what thought patterns are blocking integration. Ask them to release learned pain and transmute it. All the methods and practices mentioned in this book can be used for healing with angels. Basically, all angels are healers as well as messengers. So all healing practitioners can call upon angels for extra guidance and love.

Since angels are responsible in part for arranging coincidences, they can arrange for you to find the right doctor or healer for your particular condition. They can also rearrange your cells on a microscopic level, with the help of your own imagination. Visualize angels programming your immune system with healing messages and charging it up with energy.

When people get so sick that they are no longer in control of their own healing energy, or if something terrible happens and they end up in a coma before it is their time to die, healing angels are sent down from God to take charge. These healing angels purify the atmosphere around those who are gravely ill and unconscious. In doing this, they provide a barrier against unwanted and sickening influences. Inside the barrier, they purge the atmosphere of negativity, providing pure, clean, comfortable energy. Then the healing rays of love have direct access to the one who is ill and suffering. If you know anyone in such a state, help the angels by visualizing a healing force of angels around the person.

Healing angels do not compete with or feel prejudice against hospitals and medical doctors. Each hospital, whether it likes it or not, has its own guardian angel. Nurses have been known to see angels around humans who are recovering from grave illnesses, and doctors are often guided by divine insight. When healers recognize the role of healing angels, these healers can be more powerfully effective in what they do.

Balance of the body/mind and the spirit is the basis for healing. This is a simple concept, but it can be difficult to put into practice. So bring in the healing angels to help you.

Some books on healing are listed in Part Five. Incorporate angels into whatever you read on healing. Use your imagination, and you will discover the many ways angels can help with the healing process. Also, see Linda Zwingeberg Fickes's article in the Angel Forum.

Rescuers

Angels of the moment rescue us in various ways. If we are in grave danger of being physically injured, they will do whatever they can to help us (as long as we are not resistant). Angels of the moment sometimes appear as humans. Or they may come in full angel regalia to rescue someone from the throes of death. Occasionally, we become our higher self (or our guardian angel) and act as an angel of the moment. At these times, we may not even be aware of what we are doing or of the resounding effect we have on a situation.

I once overhead a telephone conversation at a Thanksgiving dinner celebration in which a close friend of the family was telling her sister about an angel of the moment. This friend was going through a crisis; her husband was in the hospital suffering from a stroke. To add to the stress of the situation, her husband had to be moved to a hospital in the next state (where we live). This woman was staying with her mother, and each day she was driving the freeway, which she had never done before, to be with her husband.

For a while, she wasn't aware of her husband's true condition. One day when she was feeling quite vulnerable and had driven to the hospital without her mother along for support, the doctors informed her that her husband was dying from cancer in its advanced stages. After hearing this news, the woman was left alone in a sterile, cold hallway, feeling lost and helpless. Suddenly, a beautiful young man in his twenties appeared and said, "You look like you could use a cup of coffee." She said, "Boy, could I." She went with him and had cofee. He made her feel better and even told her she reminded him of his mother, which did wonders for her (she is one of the most effective and loving mothers I know). He said he was one of a group of volunteers at the hospital and would make sure her husband was fed and looked in on when she wasn't there. After her cup of coffee with this exceptional young man, the woman felt a sense of peace and strength, which enabled her to make the drive home without falling apart. Then I heard her tell her sister that the young man just disappeared and she never saw him again. She ended by saying to her sister, "I think he was some kind of angel."

Yes, he was an angel of the moment. Was he a "real" angel who manifested in the body of a young man, or was it simply the young man's higher self being utilized in this situation? Well, whoever he was, he was a rescuer, and he gave this friend a sense of peace and well-being of the sort only angels are capable of transmitting.

Synchronism Agents

Have you ever thought that there was something more to coincidence than just random chance? Psychologist Carl Jung and physicist Wolfgang Pauli thought so, and they termed this "something more" synchronicity. Synchronicity involves the peculiar interdependent relationship of two events whose connection is apparent to the observer but whose relationship cannot be explained by the principles of causality. Such contemporaneous events seem to influence each other in ways for which we do not yet have a scientific explanation.

Jung explored the relationship between objective "chance" events and the subjective "psychic" state of the observer of these events. One of Jung's theories is that the inner and outer words are mysteriously connected, so that something happening in the outside world affects what is happening inside the inner world, or vice versa. Most theories of psychic power say that mind exerts influence over matter, or that the mind can sense or predict events that are distant in time or space.

Another possible explanation of the "something more" could be that events happening right now are part of a larger pattern that was set up earlier, or that events are being controlled by an agency in the cosmos that arranges coincidences. Such an agency might involve angels in "cosmic coincidence control."

My own view is that angels are the agents of synchronicity. Not only do angels arrange helpful coincidences, they can also use this power to send us messages. One way they communicate with us is through "synchronisms." A synchronism is a coincidence for which you recognize that strange "something more." Synchronisms are difficult to describe; they need to be experienced and explored personally.

The first step in developing your capacity to experience synchronisms is to attune your awareness of events and symbols that have meaning to you. Obviously, I have an interest in angels, and many of my synchronisms involve songs with the word *angel* in them. There is a music store that I've gone to five or six times and each time they are playing a different type of music, and each time I've heard at least one song with the word *angel* in the lyrics. Many times I have turned my radio on to find that a song with *angel* in the title is playing or that a phrase about angels is being sung at that very moment.

One way to explore synchronicity is through ANGEL® card readings (see Chapter 14), through tossing the *I Ching*, or even through tarot readings. These systems are not meant to tell the future but to make visible what is happening in the present, reflecting our state of mind and the current path we are traveling. Don't ask the same questions over and over; once is enough. (As an old saying goes, the master speaks but once.) Use tools like these as means for gaining insight only, not as a crutch for making decisions. Synchronicity can help us become more aware of what is going on in our unconscious mind.

Synchronisms are personal, and it is up to you to figure out the "something more"—the meaning. This is tricky, because how do we really know what these events mean? Be careful not to get too excited over the details of synchronisms. Don't get to the place where you are making important decisions based on deeper meanings you have read into a particular situation. Basically, I use synchronisms as an indication that I am on the right track, in the right place, for the right lesson, at the right time. The mere appearance of a compelling synchronism may itself be the message, telling you that you are playing a part in a larger pattern controlled by unseen influences.

Synchronisms are also fun, and they make life more interesting and humorous. Explore your own psychic abilities and define your own synchronistic events however you choose; there are no rules.

Humor Transformers

Many people these days are talking about transformation. Transformation means making a great change. When we ask for spiritual transformation (either consciously or unconsciously), we will get it, and we may be surprised with what this entails. When we strive for the ultimate spiritual change in our lives, tests and lessons will follow us wherever we go. The ride along the road of spiritual transformation is not always smooth, so it is important to take along your sense of humor.

The angels of transformation teach one lesson—humor. They teach us that nothing is serious and that laughing at our human selves is freedom. They teach us to laugh instead of complain. Finding humor in life is not that easy; it is much easier to be serious. Every day, we are plagued by seriousness; just turn on the evening news, and I guarantee you will soon find yourself worrying about your safety, your security, your health, your future—the list goes on and on.

Spiritual transformation is a personal choice each step of the way. Angels won't do it for us; *we* have to do our own spiritual "work." That is, only we can look inside ourselves and become aware of what we want to transform. But the angels can help us by pointing out the humor in any situation. To find the humor in a seemingly humorless situation, such as being stuck in a spiritual dilemma, stop and ask, "Okay, angels, what's so funny about this one?" We must choose a way out of every dilemma, so choose humor and call upon the humor transformers for assistance to see how funny the dilemma really is.

If you catch yourself complaining, transform your complaints into laughter. Humans are funny, especially when we complain; complaining is actually endearing if it is done with a sense of humor. It is truly amazing how many trivial things we take seriously each day; it's hilarious! What really *is* serious? What have those awful people done to you this time? Have you almost starved to death lately, or have you been threatened with jail for not paying the rent? Well, if so, try laughing; some people may think that you're a comedian out of work and buy you dinner. Then they'll find out you're about to become homeless and since you're so funny and they haven't been laughing enough lately they'll ask you to move into their place.

Do you remember the times as a child when you would be crying because of something that seemed so dreadfully serious and then all of a sudden the desire to cry would leave and you'd want to laugh but you knew that that would blow it with your parents, but you couldn't help it and burst out laughing anyway? The humor transformers are ready to restore the divine humor that will bring you into a state of grace. So when you lose your desire to be serious, let yourself *burst out laughing*; the state of grace happens in an instant.

Miracle Engineers

According to the *Oxford American Dictionary,* a miracle is a remarkable and welcome event that seems impossible to explain by means of the known laws of nature and is therefore attributed to a supernatural agency. Of course, the supernatural agency is God's crew of angels. Miracles come in many sizes and in various ways. There is a popular bumper sticker that reads: "Expect a Miracle." This is good advice for those of us who are becoming aware of angels, for angels are the engineers who organize and manage miracles.

Love is the force behind miracles. When love is converted into pure, unconditional energy, it heals whatever it touches. Miracles teach and perpetuate love. Miracles can transform those who doubt and hate into those who hope with love. Love, in and of itself, is a miracle. When angels choose insufferable human beings for miracles, they are always trying to teach them that they are loved. Think of Scrooge; he denied love every day until those spirits got a hold of him.

Each time we change our thinking from a negative to a positive program, we have brought about a remarkable and welcome event. Life is a miracle all around us, every day. When you make the choice each day to be happy and not worry, realize what a miracle it is to choose the positive. Over time, small miracles add up to large ones. Miracles do happen, and miracles teach love, unconditionally, through God's agency of miracle engineers.

Chapter 7

Angels Who Embellish Human Life

Worry Extinguishers

And which of you by worrying and being anxious can add one measure to his stature or to the span of his life?
Matthew 6:28

Angels love to destroy worry and anxiety. To worry is to torment yourself with disturbing thoughts. Worrying means you are harassing yourself with anxiety over what might happen, or over the consequences of what has already happened. Worry muddies the water of your creative nature, because it takes up too much time and energy. Worry defeats its supposed purpose by not giving you the chance to solve the problem that is worrying you. For if you are in a state of worry the problem will continue to exist, and it will own you.

If you are worrying all the time, you are taking life too seriously. Why stay up nights worrying about a problem when the solution may be available only during dream time? It's easy to fall into the trap of worrying. When you find yourself worrying at a time when you would otherwise be happy and peaceful, call on the worry extinguishers. These angels will take care of what is causing you worry, reworking every issue for the highest good of all concerned. Also, if you are worrying about a situation you have yet to face, send the worry extinguishers before you to pave the way. Then notice patterns of how everything works out. If you are running late to an appointment, the other person will be even later—so why fret on the way? "Let go and let the angels," so that you can use your time for happiness and creativity. (Part Three includes specific methods for releasing worry.)

Happiness Trainers

A father and son who live on a well-traveled highway somewhere in Illinois are called "the wavers," because all they do all day is sit in the front yard of their junk shop and wave and smile at anyone traveling down the highway. Sam Chapman and his father Clarence spend up to twelve hours a day just waving at passersby. Frequent travelers on this road say that it is a welcome treat to have the wavers wave and smile at them; they say that it changes their mood to a much lighter state. What the waving does is wake them up—wake them up to happiness, wake them out of their present state of worry and tight time schedules. Just thinking about the wavers makes me happy; I can see their smiling faces in my mind.

When asked about their job, the wavers say that they had to *train* themselves to be happy and to sit in one place and wave at people all day long. We could all use some happiness training, and luckily for us there are flocks of angels whose sole purpose is to train humans in the art and practice of happiness. These angels want to wake us up to happiness, just as the wavers wake up passing motorists. (Could it be that the wavers are angels?) Happiness without reason, regardless of the circumstances in your life, gives you an ease of being in the world. This is the ultimate freedom—to experience a state of happiness you can carry with you wherever you are, whatever you are doing, whoever is with you—the freedom to be unconditionally happy. Claiming and accepting happiness is difficult for most of us. There may be several reasons why some people can't accept happiness into their being. Quite often, they feel they have to do everything for themselves without any heavenly help. They don't realize that they can "let go and let the angels." Accepting happiness may require reprogramming or changing the way you think about life, which may involve reevaluating your priorities and beliefs; this is why we need happiness trainers. Happiness trainers help us identify the things we do that keep us from true, unconditional happiness. They make us aware of the reactions we have to situations that take away happiness. To be happy means being in a state of fascination with life, where situations are simply interesting, not necessarily good or bad.

Happiness is now; it doesn't happen tomorrow or depend on circumstances. The happiness of the past is spent, so happiness training requires full awakeness in the now. Part Three offers some specific methods for happiness training. Get to know the happiness trainers, ask them to come and help you train in the blessing of happiness, and then read about Happiness Training in Chapter 17 to guide you in developing your own working model of happiness.

If you find yourself in a serious mood, look up at the sky and visually imagine all those happiness trainers waving and smiling at you!

Fun Executives

Have you ever really thought about fun? The *Oxford American Dictionary* defines fun as that which provides lighthearted amusement and enjoyment. When we do something we like, we say, "This is fun." Sometimes, work can become play; if we like it, then it is fun. Wouldn't it be great if everything we did provided lighthearted amusement? Well, that might be taking it a bit too far, but in this day and age we definitely need more fun. Angels' work is their play. The fun executives are always ready to provide light for your heart in any situation. They get their name from knowing how to manage fun and put it into effect.

When we set aside time for fun, sometimes we don't know what to do. We might go on vacation, expecting to have lots of fun, but instead we become bored. How ironic life can be! Adults often say, "I'm too busy to have fun." Games are supposed to provide fun, and most jobs are like games—there are rules, scores, players, and goals. So why isn't work fun? Work isn't fun because we take it seriously, and serious things usually aren't fun. Fun is like happiness; it depends not on circumstances but on our being in synch with ourselves and the universe. Fun is Zen; it requires full, effortless attention to the moment. Once again, children can serve as our teachers. Watching children play can make time stand still; children are right in the moment, letting their imaginations run wild, taking cues from their friends, and creating fun. Children at play scream with glee and laughter. Angels want us to have fun—fun we can take with us to work, to leisure time, to any activity. Angels provide us with lighthearted amusement. Life is funny, especially when it is fun, and we can laugh wherever we go.

Think of a time that was really fun. It probably came unexpectedly, with people you never imagined you'd enjoy. Maybe it started out as an adventure, exploring new ground. Maybe you were by yourself, cleaning your house, and it turned out to be fun. Fun is possible anywhere, anytime; it really is. When you are in a situation that isn't fun and you want it to be, take a time-out to get into synch by relaxing into the moment. If you're suffering from boredom, then do something about it. Get out, and ask the angels for a change. Don't grow up; regress if necessary. Find that child within you and learn to play again. Fun is contagious; let it start with you and then spread to those around you.

Call in the fun executives whenever you need good, old-fashioned, childlike fun. Ask and you will receive. Whether you're at a party, at work, or on vacation, just call on the fun executives and let your imagination speak to you. Take your cues from these angelic friends who represent the true essence of fun!

Mirth Makers

Mirth is like a flash of lightning, that breaks through a gloom of clouds, and glitters for a moment; cheerfulness keeps up a kind of daylight in the mind, and fills it with a steady and perpetual serenity.

Joseph Addison

Mirth is a little different from fun, although the two often go together. Picture a large round oak table lighted by lots of candles. Around the table are a party of friends who are practicing the "eat, drink, and be merry" religion. Joyful music is playing, and the laughter is on the verge of uncontrolled hilarity, exceeding the limits of propriety and reason. Everything is amusing and thus provides an excuse to laugh and giggle. Glee, the effervescence of high spirits and ecstatic gestures, is alive at this table. Good nature, good spirits, benevolent joviality, and a sense of love for all hold reign as the sights and sounds of merriment continue. Joy, merriment, glee, laughter, and fun equal mirth.

Mirth goes a step beyond fun. Mirth is like a magic spell cast over those participating in fun. It involves the merriment of the moment, not necessarily wit and fun making. You may find the example of mirth given in the above paragraph a bit too gustatory for a book on angels, but angels understand that we are humans and that we need to eat and drink together. Angels appreciate the sense of communion we experience when we share meals with others. Mirth is meant to be shared, and angels create it to share with us. If we could see the angels at the party described, they would be dancing, giggling, and singing with joy right in the midst of all the human activity.

Of course, we don't have to be eating to be graced with mirth. Being in love or taking a long walk with the one you love can be quite mirthful. Actually, anything you do when you are in love with life can be mirthful.

It would be difficult to have mirth without the angels; it is their invention. If you need mirth in your life for you and those you love, ask the mirth makers. Mirth makers are always ready to celebrate by adding extra joy and laughter to happiness. You may need to be the instigator, so follow your heart to the gleeful side of life, to mirth.

The Cupid Force

Cupid is the Roman god of love, the son of Venus. Cupid is an angel; he is portrayed as a young angel with wings. True romantic love is the greatest gift available to humans on earth. Where do we find this greatest gift? If you go looking for it, you won't find it; it has to find you.

If romantic love is the greatest gift from heaven, why does it cause us so much trouble? One reason is that it involves other humans. Other humans cause us trouble when we expect them to provide us with happiness. Only we can generate and accept our own happiness; others can embellish our happiness, but they can't give it to us. We have to have it first. Love comes to those who already possess love. Love comes when it can multiply and create an abundance, so there is enough to give away.

Sometimes, Cupid causes us so much trouble we want to re-name him "Stupid Cupid." You have heard the saying that, under the spell of romance, "love is blind." We don't notice the obvious, until later. We attract what deep down we feel we deserve, so look at the obvious. What have you attracted? Have you attracted someone who is loving and generous in every way, or someone who is draining your peace of mind and wreaking havoc on your life?

Often, we hold on too long to someone who is not really compatible with our true self, and by holding on there is no room
for anything better to come along. Keeping an atmosphere of
freedom and release around you when you are in love opens the
channels. When we love others, we must set them free so that
they can come and go, and we must release them with forgiveness when they do something we don't like. Work on finding
your true worth, and the Cupid force will find your true love.
Don't limit Cupid by asking for someone specific. Let the angels
chose your partner; you won't be disappointed, and most likely
you'll be pleasantly surprised.

Prosperity Brokers

Prosperity is the art of being financially successful and fortunate. Prosperity doesn't mean having hoards of money; it means
that the money you have is managed in a positive way. Regardless of what we have on paper, it's the way we live that makes
us prosperous. Money is like energy: If it is used, it creates more;
if it is stifled and stored, it withers (the interest rate earned on
money in a bank often doesn't keep up with the rate of infla-
tion). To use money as energy, we cannot be attached to it. We
must be willing to release money with the positive thought that
it will continue to work for us, that the energy cycle will not
be broken. If you want freedom but you work all day with the
belief that only money will give it to you, when will you ever
have the time to be free?

Money is an apparition, a dream; if you chase after it as if
it were real, you become part of a dream, different from what
you are. This dream can become a nightmare and can cause a
person extreme detriment and desperation. The belief that having money is good and not having money is bad is limiting and
mistaken; having money is totally useless unless you have a use
for it, and if the use you have in mind is a negative one then
money can be destructive. By the same token, not having money

is a problem only at those crucial moments when money is needed. Prosperity brokers can help move those crucial moments around to the times when you have money—hence, no problem.

Call in the prosperity brokers to teach you the true essence of wealth and abundance. Wealth and abundance come from an attitude of seeing our life as its own fortune, rich and plentiful with enough to go around. With a prosperous attitude comes a knowing that the universe will take care of us. The prosperity brokers make invisible deals for you, which may involve transferring your wealth—that is, converting time, energy, and ideas into more negotiable commodities. Or they may make deals to enable you to enjoy your wealth more with love. Or they may need to teach you about gratitude, to be grateful for what you do have rather than focus on scarcities. They may teach you to be grateful for each moment as a precious gift and thankful for each situation as a valuable lesson.

There are many excellent books written about spiritual prosperity and financial abundance; some will be mentioned in Part Five. If you decide to explore this subject further, take the prosperity brokers and your guardian angel as guides and helpers with the methods written in these books. So often, in employing "the power of positive thinking," humans forget to employ angels as well. Good luck and good fortune to you!

Chapter 8

Angel Psychologists

Brain Program Editors

I've said before that angels are like thoughts and that they inspire us by instilling ideas into our thought processes and patterns. Angels would never interfere with our thought processes without our asking, so ultimately we are in charge. If we make a conscious choice to let them in, angels can help us eliminate negative and worrisome thoughts in many ways. One way is by acting as brain program editors.

If you want to be a happier person, it is important to know exactly why negative thoughts need to be edited. These are some of the ways negative thoughts affect our well-being:

1. Negative thoughts depress vitality, including the immune system.
2. Negative thoughts and statements influence other people around you.
3. Negative thoughts and ideas bias your perceptions in favor of detecting and focusing on the negative aspects of existence.

Therefore, you expect and search (consciously or unconscious-ly) for negative results to confirm your negative expectations.
4. Negative thoughts distract you from the pursuit of positive goals. For example, you might waste time and energy preparing to cope with a possible negative situation, instead of pursuing a more valuable positive opportunity.

If you are aspiring to be your higher self, changing negative thoughts and editing the programs in your brain that don't work well are valuable pursuits. If you are using creative visualization techniques to connect with the abundance in the universe, it is important to know how and why visualization and positive thinking work. The benefits come mostly from eliminating negative belief programs that make you feel undeserving of your highest good.

Brain program editors, if you allow them, can have access to your brain and mind. They can go into your brain like technicians and improve your programming. If you put yourself in a receptive state, these angels will reprogram your brain by adding new information and discarding negative and stale programs.

You might think this sounds ridiculous—letting angels into your brain to change things! Many of you, however, allow more questionable things (such as mind altering chemicals, outmoded beliefs, and T.V.) to enter your brain, so why not angels? Visualize angels having the same effect as endorphins on your brain. These methods can introduce new brain-wave forms, improve molecular structure, and program inspiring beliefs that will give you a mission of greatness in life.

Archetypal Angels

For many years, I believed that the gods and goddesses of ancient Greece and Rome were actually angels. Then I came across support for this idea in several of the books I've read on angels. Dorothy Maclean, in her book *To Hear the Angels Sing*, writes: "I realized with joy, excitement and awe that the mythological gods of Greece were members of the Angelic world. This recognition was another instance of the truth of the oneness of all life — a leavening of the coded virtues of the Old Testament with the grace and beauty of the pagan world."

Jungian psychology studies the effect archetypes have on human personality. Archetypes are inherited from universal ancestors, such as the gods and goddesses of ancient Greece, India, and Rome. Archetypes are lodged in our unconscious as patterns of ideas, thoughts, and physical images. Archetypal energy, in the form of angels, stores the original models or prototypes from which human personalities are designed. In general, all mythological beings can be discussed as angels who represent our personality drives. By understanding these aspects of our personality, we come to a deeper understanding of ourselves and our drives. If we understand the archetypes, we can use this information to fill in the blanks of our personalities and strive for greatness.

When looked at as angels, archetypes come alive as a form of guidance. Each archetype you possess has a higher aspect that can manifest under the proper conditions. Also, if you study all the aspects of a particular archetype you've inherited, you may find the clue to certain behavior patterns you want to change. Astrological signs are also archetypes, and each planet is associated with one of the archetypal gods and goddesses of ancient Rome. One way to study the various archetypes is to read about them in mythology books or to consult books on Jungian psychology.

The archetypes are not meant to limit us; they are simply personality blueprints we inherit from the universe; we can trade them in for new ones if we choose, or we can rise above their influence completely. The inheritance of personality traits in various combinations makes us unique. We can supplement our basic personality traits by calling to us an angel for an archetype we may be lacking, and we can learn to love the archetypes with which we are born and in turn love ourselves more.

Chapter 9

Angels of Nature

The Devic Kingdom

The devic kingdom is the perpetuating life force of nature. It has a hierarchy of its own. Devas are the royalty of nature; they hold the archetypal patterns of every species on earth. Devas oversee entire landscapes. The smaller nature spirits, such as fairies, elves, gnomes, wood sprites, nymphs, and fauns, are given the blueprints of various plant forms, and they become the craftspeople who tend to the smallest details of each plant. In a sense, what angels are to human beings these little spirits are to plants and animals — sources of guidance and perfection.

The devic kingdom wants to share nature with us in a harmonic way, bringing us joy through the glorious creations of flowers, trees, fields of wheat, tropical forests, and so forth. The devic kingdom helps teach us respect for the earth and its energy currents.

Have you ever been inside a building that didn't feel right for some reason? Outside, the landscape held a barren, empty feeling in places and the plants didn't seem to grow very well despite ample watering and care. On the other hand, maybe you have noticed how some houses seem to fit right into the natural setting of the land; the plant life around them is lush, and the ambiance feels "right." Or maybe you have a favorite park with these characteristics. The Chinese have a word for this subtlety: *feng-shui* (which, translated literally, means "wind-water"). When the *feng-shui* is right, there is an alignment with the wavelike *ch'i* currents of the earth. In the West, this understanding is referred to as geomancy, which is based on the premise that humans do not act upon the earth, they interact with it. The devas can help you get the *feng-shui* right in your own environment by sending you messages concerning exactly where to build and plant and how to landscape. As always, the best way to receive messages from the devas or from any angel is to pay quiet attention to your intuition. If you are planting a garden, take your time to find the right spot for it by listening to nature. Open your heart and mind to the devic kingdom, and the devas will give you creative ideas for the *feng-shui* of your place in the universe.

For more information about the devic kingdom, read Dorothy Maclean's *To Hear the Angels Sing*. This inspiring book relates messages Dorothy received from the devas on how to grow the miracle garden at Findhorn.

Chapter 10

Designer Angels

There may be some areas in your life that the angels described so far don't seem to fit. Well, no problem! You can simply ask that an angel suited to this area take over. Basically, all you have to do is define the situation and name the angel who is supposed to take charge of it. A custom-designed angel will arrive and take on the job. In this way, you can draw to you your own personal flock of angels.

Designer angels can help for a variety of situations. For example, if you are a teacher, you may want to name an angel of education to watch over and guide you. You might name the angel something like Socrates or Horace. If you are a student, you can call upon a designer angel to help you study.

If you are a writer, call in a specific angel to help you write. Give the angel an appropriate name, maybe the name of a character in your next best-seller. Also, it is always helpful to get in touch with the angel of the typewriter or word processor you use when you are writing; this angel will help you in a variety of ways. According to best-selling angel novelist Andrew Greeley, Gabriel(la) is the patron angel of electronic gadgets.

You can also call upon designer angels for help with the communication arts or communication in general. Send angels with the letters you write and the phone calls you make.

If you're an artist, you can get very specific and name angels for your paints, for certain colors you are using; you can even assign angels to your favorite paintbrush and to each masterpiece you create.

If you are a businessperson, assign an angel of profit and an angel of customer increase or customer service to your business.

Think of your hobbies and the way you spend most of your time. There's room for angels in every activity and in every moment of the day. Some angels like to cook, even though they can't eat what they create!

Assign an angel to be the guardian of your hearth and home—to create a loving atmosphere where peace prevails. You can even assign an angel to each room. Set a place at the dinner table for your home guardian and designate a place where this angel can sit in your living room.

Angels are always ready to assist in the process of birth, especially in the birth of human beings. Angels like to be included in the miracle of creation from the very beginning. Invite them in. Of course, your guardians will be there anyway, but they enjoy company.

Angels can be assigned to groups or organizations that have an objective purpose of promoting well-being. Any group with an enlightened cause, whether it be promoting healthy fun for the individuals in the group or working toward world peace, has a group mind. If you belong to a group fitting these criteria, then acknowledge the group angel. The group angel represents the group mind. You can regard the group mind angel as the guardian of the group, and you can send this angel before you. Also, be sure to ask the group angel to guide you into the group mind to work out problems and create new awareness.

In contacting designer angels, pretend that there is a big adoption agency in heaven from which you can adopt an angel or that there's a catalogue of angels you can peruse. Have fun and think of this like a "star registry," where by naming a star it becomes yours. Look up to the sky and name an angel or a flock of angels to preside over the areas of your life that make you who you are.

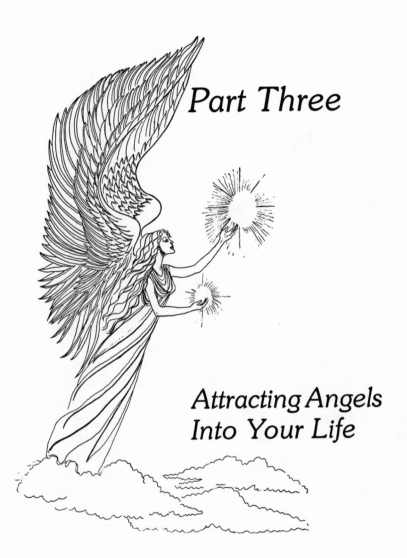

Part Three

Attracting Angels Into Your Life

About Part Three:

Keeping an Angel Journal

The main objective of Part Three is to help you clarify your goals, aspirations, and deepest desires and then discover ways the angels can help you create a sustainable positive energy (faith) toward attaining them. Angels have very creative ways to let you know they are providing what is necessary for accomplishing your ultimate mission. The key is recognizing the signs that show they are working (playing) with you through your higher self (or your own guardian angel). These signs include peace of mind, feelings of great hope, fortunate coincidences, and favorable meetings. Such signs confirm that you are on course and that your angel channels are open and fine-tuned to the universe of radiant bliss.

To employ the methods in Part Three in a personal way, it is helpful to keep an angel journal. Your angel journal will become a workbook for understanding your goals and for visualizing the future, as you learn to focus on what you want instead of worrying about what you don't yet have.

In your angel journal, you can free your imagination from the trap of seriousness. In it, you can challenge, accept, and reach

58

into the galaxy of your imagination. Your imagination is your direct line to God. Cultivating and harvesting your imagination will save you from boredom, and will help you become attuned to your intuition.

Use your angel journal as a reminder to become less serious by listing ways to take life as lightly as the angels do. Keep track of everything you discover about happiness and lightness in your journal; record sayings and excerpts from books and articles that inspire you. Keep track of all angel experiences, synchronisms, and thoughts about angels. Use your journal to discover other dimensions to your sense of humor and lightness through angel awareness.

Part Three tells you how you can work (play) with the angels to rebirth yourself into angel consciousness, where we realize that happiness is in ourselves, not in our circumstances. You will learn about how angels can guide and assist you every day of your life.

For a moment, think of life as an experiment, one that is set up for the experience of enlightenment. There is nothing you can do to bring about enlightenment; enlightenment is serendipitous—a pleasant discovery made by accident. But accidents of this kind are more likely to happen when your life is set up for conducting a spiritual experiment rather than a worldly or physical one.

Perhaps we set up the experiment before we are born, finding proper parents, locations, and other opportunities for our growth and then climbing into our bodies and growing according to our experimental guidelines. Most likely, we set high standards for ourselves, higher than we can imagine now that we are actually doing the experiment. One fortunate aspect about this experiment is that it is personal to you, and you can change the rules, take away limits, set new records, or change the course completely because you have free will. Another fortunate aspect concerning your growth experiment is that you have invisible assistants from the heavenly providence who remember the highest goals you set for this experiment. They are always there to remind you in their inspiring fashion just how wonderful and important you are. These invisible assistants are the angels.

Your life is not a serious experiment; it is a light, optimistic, and humorous experiment. By attracting angels into your life and consciousness, you will experience the radiant bliss and humor of the universe.

Chapter 11

Becoming an "Optimystic"

Becoming an "optimystic" means taking a light and hopeful view of your spiritual path. When you are an optimist, you expect good results. When you are a mystic, you seek union with God (whoever and whatever that means to you, of course). When you combine optimism with mysticism, you become an optimystic. When you take a light and hopeful view of your spiritual quest for enlightenment, you create a positive environment where good things thrive—good things such as hope, good luck, good fortune, fun, wishes that come true, dreams that are realized, wonderful visions of a paradisiacal heaven, and unconditional, blissful happiness.

Do you remember wishing upon a star as a child? Walt Disney appropriately used a song about wishing on a star as his theme song. Do you remember throwing coins in a wishing well or pond? Pulling apart a wishbone? Making a wish as you blew out the candles on a birthday cake, or blew the seeds of a dandelion to the wind? A wish is a desire or mental aim. A wish is also a blessing. You have heard people ask others to wish them luck. When you wish people luck, you express hope about their welfare and hope that they will prosper. Wishing is a way of expressing a desire. Wishful thinking means you are expecting the best to happen. Start to be aware of your wishes. You may say, "I wish I could. . . . I wish I had. . . . I wish I was . . . " quite often and not even notice that you are wishing. Wishes might not always come true the way we'd like, but often enough they come true in ways beyond what we could even imagine. Wishing is one of the optimystic's main tools.

Hope is a feeling of expectation combined with desire. Wishing will not bring you anything without a burning desire. A strong desire will set your mind in action toward attaining your goals. You need hope for your wishes and desires to come true. Bernie Siegel, who has helped many people heal themselves from cancer, says, "There is no such thing as false hope." He also states, "Optimists live longer. Pessimists have a more accurate view of the world, but they don't live longer." Becoming an optimystic changes your mental chemistry, so your thoughts are changed and the situations in your life are rearranged to fulfill your hopes, desires, and wishes. Becoming an optimystic, means you have decided to live a "charmed" life.

Another tool of the optimystic is to interpret everything that happens in a positive light. This may seem impossible, but with practice you can do it. Give yourself "good luck." That is, find good luck and be ready for it. Interpret situations as lucky, even if they seem far from it. Don't say, "This is the worst thing that could happen; this is just my luck." Figure that in some way whatever happened might have been worse. If you think you are unlucky, then you tend to find more back luck. Good luck comes from taking advantage of opportunities offered and from passing through the low times with a light and cheerful heart. Walking under ladders has always brought me luck, and I've found that wonderful things always happen on Friday the thirteenth. Max O'Rell put it this way: "Whether or not it's bad luck to meet a black cat depends upon whether you are a man or a mouse."

Magnetize good luck to your life; it's up to you. Be aware that superstitions are in opposition to angel power. If you insist on being superstitious, the angels feel that you are not trusting them. Try eliminating all superstitious behavior from your life. If you believe that doing one thing will cause another thing to happen, change your thinking, do the one thing, and see that it does not cause the other thing.

Becoming an optimystic means eliminating suffering. Suffering is not a virtue. Suffering means you are subjecting yourself to pain, loss, damage, and disadvantage. Sometimes, sufferers even take on someone else's pain if they don't think they are suffering enough on their own. Suffering and sadness are habits that afflict many of us. Suffering can teach us lessons, if we can identify what is causing the suffering and release it from our lives. God does not make us suffer; we make ourselves suffer. An optimystic knows that suffering cramps one's style, and interferes with hope and happiness. Make the choice to suffer less and fulfill hopes more.

Integrating fun and play into your spiritual pursuit and developing a keen sense of humor are other tools of the optimystic. *Lila* (pronounced "leela") is a Sanskrit word meaning the divine play of creation, or the divine play of the universe; it is the reason God created the universe. Translated, it means pure fun. (That seems like a good reason to create a universe!) Part of the optimystic's job is to promote fun and play in the universe. The seriousness of life is forever removing fun and play from view. The optimystic can reclaim play, fun, and humor and make the world a happier place. The angels want to teach us how to play and have fun, two areas of their expertise.

Mystics are known to most of us as people who have spiritual visions or intense religious experiences. Mystics see beyond the popular explanations held by their social group. The *Oxford American Dictionary* defines a mystic as someone who is initiated into the mysteries and who can transcend ordinary human knowledge using intuition. A mystic enjoys moments of spiritual ecstasy and peak experiences of love and joy. By becoming

optimystics, we can transcend the ordinary and accept the unusual in a light and happy manner. Angels will provide spiritual
ecstasy and peak experiences for us if we want them. Don't be
afraid to get carried away once in a while; getting carried away
can be a lot of fun, and it is one of the best "highs" available.
We can all become mystics in our own way by attracting angels
into our lives.

A spiritual quest for enlightenment is easier when you expect
the best and always look on the bright side. The bright side is
where the angels are, and they are always there to help you
become the optimystic you really are. Share your wishes and
dreams with the angels, and they will relay your hopes to the
highest good in the universe and help you cultivate a positive
environment where "good things" thrive.

Because you are reading this book, I can assume you are seeking spiritual growth on some level. Becoming an optimystic will
set the pace of your quest; it will help you understand the nature
of angels and the ways to attract them and to connect with their
realm. As you read about the ways to attract angels, think of
your role as an optimystic and how you will bring optimism and
mysticism to your experiences with angels.

SUMMARY

Method

Becoming an "optimystic," cultivating an environment where
wishes, dreams, hopes, good luck, and good fortune thrive. Setting the stage for the right attitude to use when practicing any
of the methods for attracting angels into your life.

Angels who can help

Guardian angels and spiritual guides, fun executives and happiness trainers, call them all in at one time or another; they are
all able to provide optimism and mystical experiences.

Tools and ideas

1. Take a light and hopeful view of your spiritual path.
2. Refamiliarize yourself with the power of wishing and of hope.
3. Cultivate and harvest good luck; interpret everything that happens as a lucky situation.
4. Suffering interferes with the spiritual growth of the optimystic.
5. Incorporate fun, play, and humor into your spiritual practices.
6. Accept and "go with" mystical visions and peak experiences of joy and love; these are the ways an optimystic has direct contact with the angels.
7. Always look on the bright side of an issue; the bright side is the home of the angels.
8. Get rid of any superstitions you may have by becoming aware of them and changing your thinking about the outcome.

When optimystics are backed by faith and imagination, they become powerful forces in the universe, forces that can change the world around them with one positive thought, idea, or action.

Chapter 12

Cultivating Imagination and Faith

Imagination is more important than knowledge.

Albert Einstein

To cultivate your imagination and faith means spending time and care developing them for harvest (use) in your life. Faith and imagination must become intimately familiar to you, because they are the main ingredients in realizing and following your truest desires. Your desires must become clearly realized in your imagination so that the seed of hope has a place to germinate. When you know what it is you want, ask for it. Asking means you've planted the seed; then you can water the seed with hope and faith. Imagine and visualize your desire in its completed form, and know by faith that it is yours.

You may be thinking that you don't have faith and imagination, but you do. Every human being has faith and imagination. They may be lying dormant from nonuse, but they are there and can be cultivated for harvest. Faith, it is said in the Bible,

66

can move mountains. Faith is *knowing*; any doubt ruins it. Concentrate on knowing, not believing. Believing has limits; it raises doubts in and of itself and always becomes an issue. But if you *know* something, you have it; it is part of you, and this is where true faith begins. (Knowing leaves the doors open to alternatives.) Faith is the ability to sustain a state of inner awareness (consciousness) and positive energy toward realizing your goals and desires in life. Faith involves keeping the energy strong enough so that worries and doubts are blocked and the channels of visualization remain open and clear. Faith is the projection of your intentions into the future. It is the assumption that things are managed so that they work out in the long run. Faith is the trust that God is unconditional.

Imagination is the art and practice of producing ideal creations and forming clear mental images. Your imagination is your future. It is the only place the future exists. When you want something, you must be able to visualize it and produce an ideal image of it in your mind. When you use your imagination with faith, you will know without effort what you want and how to attain it because you already have it in your mind. Imagination is your direct connection to the angels.

With faith, imagination, the angels, and God, you can do anything. If you are having trouble experiencing angels, use your imagination and faith to get to know their ways. Imagine everything you can about angels—what you already know and what you want to know. Imagine meeting an angel; imagine what the angel would look like, what you would talk about, and what the angel would sound like, smell like, and feel like. Visualize floating into the etheric realm and flying with the angels through all the heavenly colors. If you aren't having much luck with this, keep trying. Write about your feelings in your angel journal; describe your faith, your imagination, and your impressions about angels.

Develop your own system for knowing angels. To know is to notice, to recognize, and to feel positive. You don't have to convince yourself. There is no need for effort; just relax and pay attention. Building and developing your faith and imagination may take time, but think of it as something fun to do. Know that you will be taken care of, know that you are loved unconditionally by God, and know that you are worth it. If you have beliefs that contradict your sense of worth, work on eliminating them. (Review the section in Chapter 8 on brain program editors to help in eliminating negative programs and beliefs.)

To attract angels and get them to play for you, remember to cultivate and harvest your imagination. Then think positively and become an optimystic. Plant the seed of hope, and the angels will water it. Create your future; you already have the resources. You can create heaven; all it takes is a little harvesting.

SUMMARY

Method

Cultivating and harvesting your faith and imagination. Attracting angels by developing your imagination and faith.

Angels who can help

Call on guardian angels and spiritual guides to keep you on course; worry extinguishers to cast out doubts, fears, and worries; brain program editors to edit out negative beliefs about yourself; creativity ministers and fun executives to remove effort and force; and any angels who have entered your imagination.

Tools and ideas

1. Examine faith and imagination, think about what these powerful concepts mean to you, and write about your thoughts in your angel journal. Become one with faith and imagination; develop effortless knowing.

2. Clarify what your desires are and what you want out of life. Imagine you have what you want now (you do). Then complete the following statement: "Angels, I am asking that _____, and that the stream of faith and positive energy I have focused on this desire remain clear and constant."

3. Create the energy in your imagination for what you want and let yourself visualize it. Start a fund of energy, like an energy bank account. Deposit positive thoughts and visualizations of actual steps that can be taken for realizing your goals. (Ask the angels for a high interest rate and return on your energy.)

4. *Know* that you will be taken care of; trust the angels to connect you with the abundant loving force in the universe.

5. Use your imagination to meet an angel. Imagine everything you can about the angel, including what you would say, do, and see. Then fly with the angel up through the clouds to the heaven plane.

Things of heaven cannot be attained by perseverance; they are the grace of God. To open to this and trust in it is how belief is crystallized into faith. We cannot pay for it in any form, in any way, by our goodness, by our piety, by our great qualities, merits, or virtues; nothing. It is a gift, and all we can do is receive it.

Hazrat Inayat Khan

Chapter 13

Angel Mail

Keep on asking and it will be given to you;
keep on seeking and you will find . . .

                                        Matthew 7:7

Angels are special request agents. Special requests cover a wide
range of issues, from immediate tasks such as finding your lost
keys to help with achieving a long-term goal. When we involve
angels in our special requests, we are acknowledging the desires
of our higher self. It is fine to ask angels for help with your goals
and aspirations. You may think that angels should already know
what you want and that you shouldn't ask, but asking is the
positive step that sets the action in motion. There is no harm
in asking the angels for something, because they only do things
for the highest good of all concerned. Catherine Ponder has said,
"Your ships come in only after you have sent them out." Asking the angels for a special request is like sending your ships
and asking God to bless them. You are protected from greed with
the angels, because they see into excesses and are attuned
with your higher consciousness.

With angel mail, you write your special request on a piece of paper and mail it to the angels. The written word is said to have a special power of its own. Declaring your wishes on paper and addressing your letter to the angels is a good way of clarifying your goals and truest desires. To make a special request to the angels, simply take a piece of paper and address it to your own highest angel and the highest angels of the others whom your request involves. In your request, be specific and define what it is you want as clearly as you can. Always add the phrase "for the highest good of all concerned" to your note. Then express your gratitude. Thank the angels as if the request had already been granted. Also, thank God, and anyone else who has something to do with the request.

A story about one of the Catholic popes describes how he prayed to his guardian angel every day for guidance. When he was scheduled to confer with someone he thought might be troublesome, he would ask his guardian angel to speak with the other person's guardian angel regarding the upcoming meeting. The two guardian angels would work out the disagreements beforehand, and the meeting would proceed without needless arguments.

Apply this idea to angel mail. If there is someone in your life— your boss, your spouse, your child, your coworker, or your friend—with whom you have trouble communicating without disagreements and arguments over trivial issues, try writing to that person's guardian angel and ask that the situation be understood on the highest level. Then pay attention to what happens the next time you see the person. Look for any subtle or obvious change of heart that person suddenly has concerning the areas of disagreement.

You can use this technique whenever you feel resistance from other people. Write to their angels, and state clearly what you want from them, what it is you want them to understand, how you want them to react, and what you want them to do. By writing to a person's guardian angel, you can get past any emotional blocks either or both of you may have in the situation. Use this technique for helping those you care about to do something positive for themselves. If people you know need healing, release, love, or knowledge, write to their highest angels and ask that they be blessed with what they most need. This technique is especially useful if people you know have created situations for themselves that you can't talk about face to face. Maybe the situation involves something that you can see clearly from the outside but that they are in denial about.

When writing to angels with regard to other people, keep in mind that they have free will. We experience pain when those we love disappoint us by doing something we don't appreciate. If you have expectations about people, eventually you are going to be disappointed, one way or another. On the other hand, if you don't expect anything and give and release freely, loving others unconditionally, you will not allow their negative actions to affect you. If you are trying to influence someone romantically by writing to his or her angel, the best thing to do is bless and release him or her with unconditional love. If you are meant to be with this person, he or she will come to you freely with no conditions. The angels want you to be happy, but they also know that no other person can make you happy; you must claim your own happiness first.

You can write to any of the angels described in Part Two with special requests. You can write to the prosperity brokers for abundance, the healing angels for healing, the humor transformers for humor, and the miracle engineers for large or small miracles. Of course, you don't always have to write your requests; you can also voice them, pray them, or think them.

When you are ready to "mail" a written request, the first thing to do is to fold and seal it somehow; then find a special place for it. Some people keep their requests in books like the Bible; others use a jewelry box, their wallet, their journal, or their altar. After your request is mailed, be prepared for action. You have asked the angels, so listen intuitively for messages regarding your request, or just mail your request and forget about it until it pops into your mind again.

SUMMARY

Method

Angel mail and special requests. Attracting angels by writing to them and making special requests.

Angels who can help

Write to whichever angel is specific to your request.

Tools and ideas

1. Define your request.
2. Write your request on a piece of paper. Specify the angel to whom you are writing: for example, "to the guardian angel of _____" or "to the prosperity brokers" or "to the highest angel of _____." Somewhere in your request, include the phrase "for the highest good of all concerned." Close your request with an expression of gratitude.
3. If there are any people who might interfere with the fulfillment of your requests, write to their guardian angels and ask that anything that might block your progress with this person be removed.
4. Fold and seal your letter, find a special place for it, and consider it mailed.
5. Wait for a response, which may come in the form of intuition, opportunities for action, or feelings such as peace of mind and knowing that all is well.

Chapter 14

ANGEL® Cards

A deck of ANGEL® cards (copyright © 1981 by Drake and Tyler) consists of fifty-two very small cards. Each card has a key word representing a special essence or quality from the spiritual path. The cards are colorfully illustrated with angels in actions pertaining to the spirit of the individual cards. ANGEL® cards were developed as a part of a board game called "The Game of Transformation," which was created by the originators while living at the Findhorn Foundation. The game is a tool for exploring your inner life and consciousness. ANGEL® cards and "The Game of Transformation" are available at most New Age bookstores and are easy to order by contacting:

>   Narada Productions
>   1845 N. Farwell Ave.
>   Milwaukee, WI 53202

ANGEL® cards can provide an effective means for bringing angelic essence into your life. Some of the key qualities listed in the deck are joy, humor, peace, light, surrender, and trust. There are also two blank cards, which can be used to request a specific quality or essence not included on the other cards, or you can use them to ask the angels to send you a gift from the universe.

Right away, you can probably think of several ways to use the cards. There are no rules, but it is best not to ask about the same situation over and over again. (Again, the master speaks but once.) The cards reflect what is presently happening in your internal and external reality, and the list of key words contains nothing negative or dark. Keeping this in mind, here are some suggestions for using ANGEL® cards as tools for spiritual growth.

The first thing to do is find a quiet place to sit where you can spread the cards out in front of you. You may want to place them systematically into rows or just swirl them all around. Make sure they are face down so that your unconscious mind has a chance to come through. Or hold them fanned out in your hand, letting your energy run through the whole deck. Then pick the cards when you are ready.

To begin with, you may want to do a reading on your present state of affairs. Think about eight areas or situations in your life for which you would like guidance from the angels. I write down the following eight domains and life issues as follows:

The past
The present
The future
A gift from the universe
Love/romance
Money/prosperity
Work/career
Play/Recreation

Then I focus my thoughts on each area and pick a card when I feel ready. You may want to add or subtract areas to make the reading more personal. After you have picked the cards and written them down, study the reading for clues to any actions or breakthroughs the key words represent. You may want to leave the reading for a day or two and then return to it.

Think of a situation or question in your life for which you want guidance. It can be anything from money to love. Or ask for a reading of what is in the forefront of your consciousness, with no specific question in mind. Or ask for a set of gifts to develop in your present state of consciousness. Concentrate on your situation and pick one card to be the "trump card"; set it aside and don't look at it. Now, pick three more cards and turn them over. Think about what they mean to you and then turn over the trump card. The trump card represents an overall guiding light for the situation. Write the essences down in your angel journal and reread it in the future when you want more insight.

Do a "virtue request" with your ANGEL® cards. Look through the cards and pick out the ones representing virtues you want or need in your life. Then study the cards and the pictures drawn on them; meditate and ask for insight on these virtues. Write them down and declare this request to the angels, and be ready to explore your virtues.

Pick an angel of the day, year, month, cycle, birthday, or season; pick an angel for any special occasion you want to lighten up.

Pick an angel to help with an obstacle to be overcome; to help with a new venture, a new relationship, or a new house; or to bring inspiration and creativity to your work, schooling, and play.

Remember to have fun and keep the experience light so that the angels can truly respond. If you get stuck on what a card means to you, sometimes it is helpful to look the word up in a dictionary for insight into the word itself. The two blank cards can be very significant, because with them you can ask for something specific or for a gift from the angels or for a clean slate for the future. Invite the angels to join with you in celebrating your spiritual growth, and use the cards to communicate with them.

I showed the ANGEL® cards to a very creative and brilliant friend of mine, and he came up with a game based on the card game "War." The name isn't very appealing, but you can ignore it. The game is played with two people. First, shuffle the cards and deal them out face down. Each player turns over one card each time. With the two cards facing up, you must decide between the two of you which virtue or essence is "more important." The player with the "more important" card gets to take both cards. After the cards have been used up, the player with the most cards win. Of course, this game could stir up a few healthy arguments, so it is important to keep it a fun learning experience.

My first experience with ANGEL® cards was very memorable. I had seen the cards several times in my favorite bookstore, but I had never bought them because I was skeptical of what they might represent. I waited until my best friend and witness came to visit me for a vacation, and the first thing we did was to buy a deck of the cards. We opened them in the car and the first one we picked was a blank card, so we asked that our vacation week be filled with synchronisms (it was!). We weren't really sure what to do with the cards at first, and then we came up with the idea of giving them out wherever we went that week.

We had a great deal of fun leaving cards with tips in restaurants and handing them out to friendly people up and down the coast of Virginia and North Carolina. We also gave them to people we knew, and we had friends pick out a card without looking. Giving ANGEL® cards to people led to many discussions about angels. So we had an angel-filled week of fun, lightness, and synchronistic events.

The cards we gave to friends turned out to be very meaningful in their lives, as they later told me. To give is to receive, so giving the cards gave us much in return.

For more information on "The Game of Transformation" and to find out about the Facilitators' Training Workshops offered by InnerLinks (which include extensive work with the ANGEL® cards and with angels in group settings), please contact:

Kathy Tyler
InnerLinks
P.O. Box 16225
Seattle, WA 98116

Chapter 15

Holding an Angel Conference

A conference is a meeting for discussion. When people know where they are going and why, they can become powerful forces in the universe. And when people are on a straight course, angels can cooperate with them in a more complete way. To help us know where we are going and to help us explore the reasons for going there, we can call an angel conference to chart out our goals and discover how the angels can help us achieve them.

An angel conference can be thought of as a chance to develop a business plan for your life. If you think about it, each human life is like a business (some small and some large), and like every business a human life needs a plan stating goals for the future. Calling a conference with the angels is a way to plan for your future, to define what you want to accomplish, and to recognize key people in your life. Angels act as your consultants and your staff of employees. The conference is a way to assign tasks that your staff can handle for you. It is also a way of defining what may be limiting your creativity or free time.

First, define your board of directors. A sample board of directors may include your version of God; Mary, Jesus, or particular saints you like; important archetypes, gods, or goddesses; ancestors or personalities from the past who intrigue you; spirit guides, gurus, biblical characters, superheroes, and sages; and so forth. Your board of directors will be inspirational, and it will be personal to you. Think of your board as an association of spiritual advisers and consultants who can help you carry out the main purpose (essence) of your business (life).

Napoleon Hill, the author of *Think and Grow Rich*, held an imaginary council meeting with his group of "Invisible Counselors" at night before going to sleep. His council was comprised of nine men whose lifework most impressed him. The object of these meetings was to reshape his character by trying to imitate these nine great men in some way. Hill wanted to become a composite of these men (see the section on soul angels in Chapter 5.) In his imaginary council meeting, Hill was able to sit among great men and dominate the group by serving as chairman. This idea can be incorporated into the angel conference.

To hold an angel conference, it helps to have a chart to follow. I take a piece of paper and draw a circle with a compass so that I end up having a mandala with sections. In the sections, I write down goals for specific areas of my life. Then I assign angels to help in the realization of these goals and desires. I also assign angels to keep certain people from interfering, so that a barrier of protection is formed. If there are people who can help you, this is a good time to address their highest angels.

The Angel Conference Diagram is an example of one form I designed for use when holding an angel conference. I also make up other forms, and sometimes I don't use a form at all. You can design one that works for your own needs. You might want to keep your forms with your angel journal and date each one so you can monitor your progress.

Angel Conference Diagram

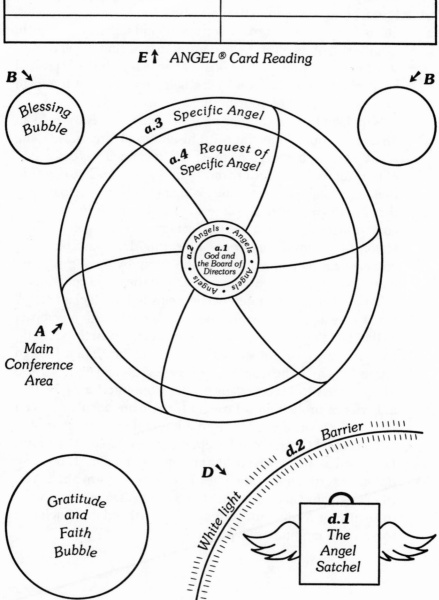

E ↑ ANGEL® Card Reading

B ↘

Blessing Bubble

a.3 Specific Angel

a.4 Request of Specific Angel

a.2 Angels • Angels • Angels • Angels •

a.1 God and the Board of Directors

↙ B

A ↗
Main Conference Area

D ↘

White light

d.2 Barrier

d.1 The Angel Satchel

Gratitude and Faith Bubble

C ↗

KEY TO ANGEL CONFERENCE DIAGRAM:

A = The main area for your conference. I write God in the center circle (**a.1**), and I also write in the names of the members of the board of directors. In circle **a.2**, outlining **a.1**, I write in the word "Angels" a few times. In the space (**a.3**) on the edge of the large sections, I define the angels for whom I have specific requests. In the large section (**a.4**), I write in my specific requests, goals, or objectives.

B = The blessing bubbles. In these bubbles, I ask the angels to bless special situations and humans.

C = The gratitude and faith bubble. In this bubble, I ask for faith and thank the angels and God and myself and anyone else for the realization of the goals of the conference.

D = The angel satchel section. This section is used to keep other humans (or other aspects of yourself) from interfering or blocking your progress. You can also use this technique to avoid people you fear and loathe. When you use this satchel (**d.1**), repeat the affirmation, "There is no such personality in the universe." Then put the name of the person who owns that personality in the satchel. *This does not mean that you want anything bad to happen to him or her!* On the contrary, it means that the angels are in charge now and that they will make the energy positive. Basically, the barrier means that you are not going to acknowledge the part of the other person's personality that conflicts with yours. Also use this area to write in any blocks you might encounter from yourself, such as fear, doubt, procrastination, and resignation. On the border of this section (**d.2**), you can write the words "White Light" or you can write the affirmation to the archangel Michael: "Divine light of the highest order under the protection of the archangel Michael." This gives you protection and sends the light of transformation to the person in question.

E = The ANGEL® card reading. You can number the sections to correspond with the sections of the main conference. Pick a card to represent an essence you can bring to enlighten the situation or request of each section.

You can convene an angel conference any way you choose. Sometimes, just starting out with a blank piece of paper and being spontaneous is a fun way to hold a conference. Also, if you have an active imagination, you can do the whole process in your head using visualization techniques.

There are no mandatory conditions for holding angel conferences. You can hold them anywhere, anytime, anyhow, but keep in mind that angels are not to be worshipped. They appreciate ceremonies, but they do not want to be worshipped; they only want to assist and help without interfering in human free will. With this in mind, here are some ideas to use for getting in the spirit of the angel conference:

1. An angel conference is not a serious and confining ritual; it is a chance to be light and to connect with the beauty surrounding angels.
2. Angels love candlelight, so light some candles for the conference (white or pink candles are especially nice for an angel conference).
3. Surround yourself with beauty, setting up a table with flowers, pictures, incense, rocks, and angel figurines to provide a nice setting for the angel conference.
4. A recording of harp or flute music is nice to play during a conference.
5. After the angel conference is complete, do a reading with ANGEL® cards. If you have several categories, pick a card for each one. Do an overall reading of the conference for additional insight.
6. Incorporate anything that will promote happiness, beauty, peace, lightness, and love into your conference.
7. Angel conferences are meant to be light and humorous, so laugh as much as you like. Invite the mirth makers and humor transformers to attend.
8. Hold the angel conference with a friend, so that you have a witness and someone who will giggle with you.

9. Pay the angels who attend with wages by doing something nice for yourself and those around you. Plant a flower garden, paint a beautiful picture, or give love and lightness away, and the angels will consider themselves well paid for their services as consultants on your staff.

10. For updates on the main conference, hold special meetings with specific angels whose help you are requesting. For example, if you need extra help in the area of career and finance, have a "power lunch" or breakfast meeting with the angel you have assigned to this domain. Take notes during the meeting if you like, and make it as real as possible. If you go out in public for the power lunch, ask for a quiet and private booth.

Chapter 16

Adventures in Antiseriousness

Not a shread of evidence exists in favor of the idea that life is serious.

Brendon Gill

People can waste a lot of time taking life seriously and worrying about perceived problems. My friend Charlie reached a period in his life when he felt burdened by problems and worries. He spent most of his time seriously worrying over what he was going to do. While driving on some treacherous mountain curves one day, pondering over the serious issues he faced, he took one curve too fast and found himself looking down several hundred feet of mountain with his van up on two wheels. In that instant, Charlie realized that he was probably going to die and that all the situations he was worried about would never be resolved. Then a sudden force (his guardian angel, no doubt) pulled Charlie's van back into control, and he was saved from imminent death. After the shock subsided, he found himself

84

laughing hysterically at how absurd his worrying was. Nothing seemed so serious anymore; suddenly, he was struck by how funny everything was, and he laughed and laughed. Charlie realized that the moments he had spent worrying were wasted time, which could just as easily have been spent in enjoyment.

Those of us who become consumed with the illusion of seriousness in our lives usually reach a turning point. Sometimes this turning point happens dramatically, as in a near-death experience; other times, it happens less dramatically, as in a sudden realization that you have spent weeks and months without having any fun. If you are not planning to have a near-death experience any time soon but you are plagued by seriousness, pay attention to the time and energy you spend on seriousness. Start by writing down all the serious issues you are dealing with in your life at the moment. Now look at how funny these issues look on paper, and let yourself laugh out loud. If the issues don't strike you as funny and you can't bring yourself to laugh, just look for some aspect of humor and lightness, however small. Sometimes when we start laughing at our lives, we end up hysterical, and we may cry, scream, or shout out the window. The point is we need a release now and then and laughter is a good one.

Give up, give in, and let go. Pretend that you are filled with helium and that the only thing keeping you on the ground are the serious issues in your life; let yourself rise above them for a different perspective. If you saw the movie *Mary Poppins*, think back to the scene with the song "I Love to Laugh"; the more people laughed, the higher they rose until they reached the ceiling. When they wanted to come down, they had to think of something sad and heavy. Take a break from the seriousness of life; the angels will encourage it. Remember G. K. Chesterton's words: "Angels can fly because they take themselves lightly."

Laughter has many benefits. It exercises the lungs, releases superfluous energy, bathes your being in endorphins (natural pain relievers), and promotes healing. (See *Anatomy of an Illness* by Norman Cousins.) If you need help bringing laughter into your life, start by surrounding yourself in humor. Do your own study on humor. Make a list of the movies, comedians, television shows, books, friends, and situations that make you laugh, and always search for more.

In your angel journal, keep track of the humor and seriousness in your life. If you catch yourself becoming plagued by seriousness, examine your behavior and that of others. Find out what keeps happening in your life that isn't funny. Whenever you like, ask the angels to release you from seriousness and connect you with humor. The plague of seriousness is everywhere: in our churches and schools, on the news, and at work. It is hard to escape from it. But there is always a way to introduce humor into any situation, and you may need to be the instigator.

Keep a page in your journal labeled "trasn bag" and draw a trash bag on the page. Whenever you have a nagging worry or negative thought you want to release, write it into the trash bag. If other people are causing you grief, put them in the trash as well. Bad habits, seriousness, complaints, and anything that disturbs your peace of mind belongs in the trash. When the bag is full, or on a weekly basis, call the angel trash collectors for a pickup. These trash-collecting angels will take your trash bag to the universal transmutation dump. If you are truly willing to part with the contents of the bag, the energy will come back to you clean and charged with a positive force to use for something creative. The angel rubbish collectors can turn one person's trash into another person's treasure. Form a clear visual image of your trash bag being carried away into the universe for the highest good of all concerned and say, "Good riddance!" Another way to take out the trash is to burn the trash bag page, and as the smoke rises visualize yourself free of all the trash you've accumulated.

Angels are antiserious; there is no weight in their realm, and they simply can't take anything seriously. This means that they can't take us or our problems seriously either. This doesn't mean they will ignore our problems; they will do what they can to help us remove the serious worries so that we can solve problems creatively and take ourselves lightly. The *Oxford American Dictionary* defines serious as solemn and thoughtful, not smiling, not casual or lighthearted, causing great concern, and of grave and somber disposition. How could anyone want to be serious after reading that?

SUMMARY

Method
Adventures in antiseriousness. Attracting angels by lightening up your load of life issues.

Angels who can help
Humor transformers, fun executives, and worry extinguishers are all antiserious; call on any of them.

Tools and ideas
1. List all the serious issues you face at the moment, and laugh at them.
2. Take a laughter inventory, and find new ways to laugh. Also, learn how to have a good hearty laugh as often as possible.
3. Keep a trash bag page in your angel journal for serious trash such as worries, negative thoughts, and negative personalities that you want removed from your life. Then take out the trash.
4. Cultivate lightness in your life.

Chapter 17

Happiness Training

Happiness is not in our circumstances but in ourselves. It is not something we see, like a rainbow, or feel, like the heat of a fire. Happiness is something we are.

John Sheerin

How many times have you heard yourself or someone else say, "When this happens, I'll be happy"? Well, it doesn't work that way; you must first be happy now—without reason. Happiness without reason is the ultimate freedom. This freedom from conditions and contingencies means that you aren't waiting for the right ingredients to make you happy; you just *are* happy. No matter what the circumstances, you feel blessed and happy. If you are truly happy without reason, you are freed from the domination of outward conditions. You are free to live happily in the present tense, in the now.

Happiness without reason requires training. The state of happiness requires that you know yourself and that you identify precise moments when you switch from being happy and at ease on this planet to being uncomfortable and out of synch.

The problem with true happiness is that there is no key to its door, there are no rules to follow no steps to take, and no conditions for it to exist. There is no manual or cookbook with recipes to read. True happiness is a state of grace. It's a bit like having a naturally occurring chemical in your bloodstream that feeds your brain and bathes your soul in positive energy. There is nothing to swallow, breathe, look at, smell, or do to become happy. Happiness comes and goes. We cannot plan it; it is a naturally occurring product of living in the present tense, free from external conditions. We can, however, train ourselves to be *available* and *open* to happiness.

Happiness training is accepting everything the angels have to teach: humor, love, beauty, lightness of being, and joy. It requires living in the now and being *awake*. You must get off autopilot. Autopilot is a personality program some of us adopt to avoid pain and to avoid living and experiencing the now. By subscribing to set routines and predictable patterns, some people are sleepwalking through the day. You won't find these people rocking the boat or moving and shaking the world; that isn't safe in their minds. Going on autopilot does not get rid of the pain and suffering in your life; it only delays and diffuses it. Sooner or later, the voids will come back to haunt the person on automatic pilot. When we see children on autopilot, we call it mental illness. Young children normally don't resist life. When they feel like crying, laughing, screaming, or singing, they just do it. Angels and children go together; they are happy and creative. Angels see this happy state as the way we are meant to be (all of us). Step number one of happiness training is: Get off autopilot. Wake up and experience your senses. Stop and smell the roses; wake up and smell the coffee.

Happiness (or unhappiness) is largely a result and function of how we *relate* and *react* to events in our lives; it does not reside in the circumstances or the events themselves. Overreacting to an adverse event makes it worse. Overinterpreting circumstances with an attitude of what should be according to a given set of conditions is a sure way to deter happiness. We must not react with fear, anger, or disappointment to the events of the day. Choose to see whatever arises in the moment with fascination and interest, and know that it is neither good nor bad. Events and things are only bad or wrong when they are compared to a standard in your imagination of what should be. Step number two of happiness training is: Don't overreact, overinterpret, or compare. Adopt a sense of lightness and humor in every situation you encounter, and the angels will be there to help.

The happy mind is free of judgments, expectations, and worries concerning other people. Other people's actions can only hurt us when we have a preconceived notion of their intent toward us. When we are happy with ourselves, then we can see others as innocent. If someone sends you a carton of horse manure, just assume they forgot the horse! Worrying about people doesn't help them or you. Expecting people to act certain ways will only disappoint you. Judging yourself and others is a waste of time. Step number three of happiness training is: Don't let other people affect your happiness. Just as events are neither good nor bad, the same is true of people; see people and their actions as interesting and fascinating, originating from a source of innocence.

You must be willing to give up suffering and worrying. Suffering is the opposite of happiness. Many people have resigned themselves to live with low-grade, chronic suffering. This suffering may stem from physical pain, mental anguish, regrets, bad habits, or emotional blocks. Whatever the cause, the result is constant suffering. Angels are frustrated with suffering because until humans are willing to give it up angels can't work their magic. When you discover a cause of suffering and worry, and you are willing to give it up, get in the habit of stopping and releasing. Stop and release; you can repeat this process in your mind and visualize the angels taking your suffering away. Once the decision to stop suffering is made, angels jump in for the transformation; whether the transition is from sickness to health or from bondage to freedom, the angels are waiting to help. The change can happen in an instant. Make peace with yourself so that if anything is making you suffer it will be gone, and you will be available to experience happiness without reason. Your suffering teaches only a temporary lesson; don't keep it around longer than needed. Step number four of happiness training is: Recognize what is causing you to suffer and work on giving it up so that the angels can help you become one with happiness. Stop worrying about yourself and others. "Let go and let the angels."

Go and love some more. Giving love on any level is a sure way to happiness. This love must be unconditional love, of course, and as always with giving you receive. Anne Frank once said, "Whoever is happy will make others happy too. He who has courage and faith will never perish in misery!" Have the courage and faith to spread your happiness and love around, and you will create an abundance that will continue to give throughout the universe. Love and happiness are synergistic; their combined effects exceed the sum of their individual effects. Step number five of happiness training is: Be generous with your love and happiness; spread it throughout the universe.

Training yourself to be available and open to happiness without reason requires that you remove obstacles such as those discussed above. Unconditional happiness is the ultimate freedom. It doesn't require that you live anywhere special, that you dress a certain way, that you ingest a mind-altering substance, or that you do anything other than make yourself available to receive it, anytime and anyplace. Happiness has been described as a butterfly; when you pursue it it is always just beyond reach, but if you sit quietly it may alight upon you. Angels are natural happiness trainers, so sit down quietly and ask them to help you develop a habit of happiness.

SUMMARY

Method

Developing a habit of happiness, so that the angels will be able to play effectively in your life. Use the steps of happiness training to recognize the precise moment you become uncomfortable and unhappy, and then change the way you think of the situation so that the angels can jump in and make you one with happiness. Write out a declaration of happiness in your angel journal.

Angels who can help

Call on your guardian angel, the happiness trainers, worry extinguishers, mirth makers, humor transformers, and cheerleaders.

Tools and ideas

1. Wake up and stop any automatic behavior that keeps you from experiencing life. Autopilot behavior is a way of resisting life and avoiding pain; it avoids the present.
2. Do not overreact to or overinterpret situations that come your way. Compare them only with themselves; in this light, they are neither good nor bad, and you can find them interesting and fascinating—and therefore positive in some sense.
3. Don't let other people's behavior interfere with your happiness. Perceive others as innocent, and adopt an attitude of optimism regarding their intentions. They are neither good nor bad, just interesting and fascinating. In most situations, people and circumstances can only hurt you if you let them.
4. Discover the causes of your suffering and worry, and be willing to give them up; the angels will step in and help you. When you feel uneasy and out of synch, stop and release whatever is blocking you.
5. Love and do as you will. Give from your abundance of happiness. As David Grayson says, "Make one person happy each day and in forty years you have made 14,600 human beings happy for a little time at least."

The quotation that follows is from Barry Stevens's book *Burst Out Laughing*. Stevens once received a rejection letter for one of her books that stated, "You write like an angel, but you just won't say the right things."

I choose to give up suffering.

This dosen't say the same thing as I choose to be happy.
One is a negative.

The other is a positive. Always be positive! But then I start
with a picture in my head of what happiness is and I limit
myself before I start.

Whereas when I choose to give up suffering – a strongly
positive act, I see now that I have written it – I notice when
I am suffering, look into the cause of it in myself, and give
up whatever makes me do it, leaving the space wide open to
whatever comes in. It isn't easy, but surely is a ladder
to heaven.

Of course, I'm also giving up luxury – the luxury of feeling
sorry for myself. I am then one step beyond where feeling sorry
for myself is possible, seeing the whole thing clearly.

I burst out laughing.

Barry Stevens

Chapter 18

Light-Heart Training

A light heart lives long.

William Shakespeare

Light-heart training teaches you to attract angels by becoming angelic. Think of light-heart training as a process of growing feathers! Being angelic is a sure way to attract angels (birds of a feather flock together). As we know, angels take themselves lightly, but what can this do for us? Simply put, developing a light heart brings out our natural ability to be entertaining, charming, and clever, and allows us to rediscover our innate sweetness. Most children have all these qualities working for them, unless something awful is happening in their lives. So this means that most of us were charming, clever, entertaining, and sweet at one time in our lives. Some of us still are!

Essential angelic qualities come to the surface only when we are authentic and genuine. Radiating sweetness and light brings you more of the same. Being authentically charming and sweet will energize those around you. Have you ever noticed those special individuals who can enter a room full of people and put everyone at ease? A true social genius makes others feel comfortable and important, regardless of their social status. Why? Because he or she is genuinely interested in people. Have you ever met someone you thought was truly charming and interesting, only to realize later that *you* did all the talking? True charm involves listening to someone and noticing the dimensions of that person's personality. Human beings *are* fascinating. Anyone living on this planet for more than a couple of years has a fascinating story or two to tell. All people on this earth have something very special and interesting to teach us. If we get bored around people, it is not because they are intrinsically uninteresting; it is because we have lost our ability to find fascination in every moment.

The key elements of lightness training are charm, sweetness, a sense of humor with an infectious laugh ready to erupt anytime, and wit—the ability to see the humor in a situation. These key elements are all interdependent.

Charm can be defined as the power to arouse love and admiration. Charm makes you attractive and fascinating, influencing others as if by magic. The *Oxford American Dictionary* defines magic as a mysterious quality that seems to enchant. To enchant means to delight completely, to enrapture with joy—literally, to encircle in song. A truly charming personality is magical and mysterious, and has an alchemical effect on the surroundings. Above all, charm attracts people to you because you are genuinely interesting and engaging. Charm also attracts angels.

Innate sweetness is another element of lightness. A sweet personality will attract angels, and a bitter one will repel them. Think about sweetness. It is agreeable, fresh, unsalted, and kind without effort. When it is artificial, we say it is saccharine, too sweet, a substitute for something real, with a bitter aftertaste. But when sweetness is integrated and real, it is purely delightful. We all have it in us. Just smile and think of something sweet like the fragrance of a flower, and you will instantly become sweeter.

Having a sense of humor and wit is the essence of a light heart.

There is, however, a very fine line between making fun and true wit. Both find the absurd and the ridiculous in life, but wit does this in a comfortable way so that no one is offended. Being witty and having a sense of humor do not mean you are making fun of anyone. Ridicule is not charming, even when you are ridiculing yourself. Ridicule makes people very nervous and uncomfortable. The source of true wit comes from a basic love of life; it is not meant as an attack on anything or anyone. Being witty means having the ability to combine words and ideas in a clever way that appeals to the intellect. On the other hand, a sense of humor does not necessarily mean that *you* have to be the one who creates humor. It means you have the ability to perceive and enjoy amusing situations, and the ability to have a good laugh. Having true wit or a true sense of humor is charming, because both bring out the best in others and lighten any heart.

The following qualities never make for a charming personality at any time, ever:

1. Criticizing means to find fault, looks for flaws, and form negative judgments. There is no such thing as "constructive criticism" unless someone is sincerely asking you for a critique, in private, and even then it is hazardous. If you engage in criticism of *anyone* in other people's presence, people will wonder what awful things you are saying about them when they aren't present.

2. Pointless complaining (or bitching) means talking in a futile, negative vein. No one but your best friend or therapist should have to listen to pointless complaining. In a group situation, complaining is totally uncalled for, and the angels will definitely make themselves scarce if you indulge in this unpleasant behavior.

3. Boredom is never welcome or necessary. If you are bored with people or a situation, the best thing you can do is to leave.

4. Tattletale behavior or ganging up on someone is terribly un-

charming. On the other hand, defending someone who is being attacked in a diplomatic way (dissolving the attack) is quite charming and clever (if you can do it right).

5. Be wary of talking politics and religion in your social circle. If such a discussion gets out of hand, be the one to change the subject.

Think of a truly charming person you know, one who is a social genius. I'll bet he or she rarely falls into any of the traps mentioned above. You may think I'm sounding a little like Miss Manners, but there are a lot of people who could use some coaching in manners. A charming manner will bring you good favor, which in turn will bring you good fortune. Charm seems to be dying out on this planet, so help keep it alive; give to the charm fund by becoming a person you yourself would like to be around.

Above all, remain true to yourself. When you are truly authentic, your charming side comes to the surface. Having a light heart leads to freedom, for it means that you are on the lighter side of life. When a heart is light, you can almost see the angels surrounding it. Ask the angels to follow you into any situation, and keep your heart light.

So shall you find favor, good understanding, and high esteem in the sight of God and Man

Proverbs 3:3–4

SUMMARY

Method

Light-heart training. Enhancing one's charm, sweetness, and wit — in essence, becoming like an angel to attract more angels.

Angels who can help

Your guardian angel, the mirth makers, the happiness trainers, the cheerleaders, the fun executives, and the muses can all help.

Tools and ideas

1. Know the key elements of lightness: authentic charm, sweetness, wit, and humor. These key elements put people at ease and create comfort in any situation. Know that they must stem from a ground of love.

2. Be aware of the difference between true wit and humor, and the barbs of making fun of someone or something. When you make a conscious choice to find more humor in your life, the angels will help you systematically. If you are stuck in a situation that seems to lack humor—for example, in a long line that doesn't seem to be moving—turn to the person next to you and say something light and funny. It takes practice and a conscious effort to find the humor in life.

3. Eliminate the following from your behavior: criticism (it is never constructive), pointless complaining, boredom, and attacking or tattletale behavior. Avoid contentious topics of discussion in groups. When you train yourself to be aware of the critic within, you can train the critic to remain silent.

4. Maintain your integrity, and be authentic at all times. (If you detect any of the nasty behaviors mentioned above in yourself, don't cover them up; *eliminate them.* That way, you can be genuinely charming and pleasant.)

5. When you "make an entrance," do it with an entourage of angels.

Chapter 19

Declarations to the Angels

You shall also decide and decree a thing and it shall be established for you, and the light [of God's favor] shall shine upon your ways.

Job 22:28

When people make declarations, they are stating clearly and formally what it is they want known. Making a declaration to the angels means that you are openly announcing what you want known to heaven. Declaring your goals and statements of things to come will establish a plan of action with the angels. A declaration can be an outline or map that you can follow. The angels will bless the declaration and add higher inspiration and aspirations to it. There are many ways to create a declaration to the angels. In this chapter, I will expand on three declaration ideas that I have used with success.

The first is a declaration to abolish stale patterns, limiting beliefs, and negative brain programs. (First of all, read about brain program editors in Chapter 8 to familiarize yourself with the ways angels can help change programs and eliminate negative behavior.)

If there is something we want to change about our personality or a habit we want to get rid of, then we can openly announce our willingness to change in a written declaration. Just the act of being willing opens a new awareness channel in your brain to detect those elements that contribute to the behavior you want to change. With this awareness, you can choose something different.

List any behavior patterns, negative brain programs, or bad habits you want to change. If you have a clear idea of any actions you can take to end them, list these as well. Now formulate a statement of your intention to end the behaviors and replace them with positive behaviors or patterns. Use this formula: "I, _____, formally and willingly choose and am open to change. I would like to eliminate the following behaviors and patterns from my life: [fill in your list]. I also agree to take action in the form of [put your list of actions here] to help facilitate my progress. I ask that a new awareness channel be established in my brain to detect the patterns when they start so that I can choose a different way of being and so that I can see how or if I have been limiting myself and sabotaging my progress. I hereby ask the angels to bless this declaration and to instill positive inspiration in place of the stale patterns that were detracting from my happiness. I ask that these angels in particular be on hand to guide me in the right direction: [list specific angels whose help you desire]." End by formally thanking the angels and the higher power in the universe, and know that you are blessed.

A second possible declaration is to state goals, desires, and hopes for the future—creating a map or outline to follow. For this declaration, you can write a formal letter to the angels, stating the path you are going to take and the quality of life you expect. Your letter can go something like this:

Dear Angels [and other interested higher parties, including yourself],

I will live a long, healthy, and prosperous life. I will create peace and harmony, and I will be blessed with the grace of happiness.

I will follow through with my lifework [describe] and see it come to pass with success and abundance. [Now add the details: the goals, accomplishments, and rewards you desire.] I will release any fear, worry, and attachment that is holding me back. I will be open to the gifts of the universe. My work will be for the highest good in the universe. All limiting thoughts are now replaced with loving thoughts of abundance.

Yours truly,
[your name]

Get as flowery as you want and have fun with it. Create an agenda or itinerary to follow, including specific dates. And, as always, remember to thank the angels. Finally, make sure you really want the things you put in your letter!

A third kind of declaration you can make involves composing a "let go and let the angels list."

Casting the whole of your cares — all your anxieties, all your worries, all your concerns, once and for all — on Him; for He cares for you affectionately, and cares about you watchfully.

Peter 5:7

A "let go and let the angels list" is a declaration to release cares and worries that you want out of your life. It's a very simple procedure. Just make a list and after each item write or say, "Yours." Your list can be as simple or as specific and detailed as you would like; either way, the angels will hear you. For example:

Dear Angels,

I am asking you to take over the following situations and work them out for my highest good:

Money anxieties: Yours
Moving question: Yours

"Bad back" problem: Yours
Health in general: Yours
Career: Yours
Fun: Yours
Disagreement with _____: Yours
Car troubles: Yours

Thank you, angels, for taking over these situations. Thank you for finding the highest solutions and guiding me in pursuit of higher ground without petty worries.

Sincerely,
[your name]

Check the declarations you have written every once in a while. Monitor yourself and congratulate yourself or any progress. You may need to update or change things, so go ahead. Yes, you can change the declarations. They are not set in stone—only on wings. One time, my friend and I had to make a formal apology to the angels for asking so adamantly for something we ended up not really wanting. Of course, the angels didn't mind because they understand human nature, but we wanted them to know that we recognized how funny and silly we had been.

Chapter 20

Bedtime Angel Review

Once asleep man has no real freedom of choice. His entire slumber is dominated by his last waking concept of self. It follows, therefore, that he should always assume the feeling of accomplishment and satisfaction before he retires in sleep.

Neville

My three-year-old niece once told me not to worry about how late she was staying up because when she finally went to bed she would go to sleep with two angels. I asked her about the two angels, and she explained that they fly all around her bed, keeping the monsters and ghosts away from her so that she can get a good night's sleep.

Sometimes our days are filled with monsters in the form of worries, stress, hostile people, and work deadlines. When we go to sleep still carrying these monsters, dream time can be a battleground. Humans need sleep because of gravity. We have a constant force field keeping us from floating off the planet, and just by standing up we are working against this force. We need sleep to recover from the day's gravity and seriousness. Thus, it is of the utmost importance that we allow our sleep time to be as calming as possible. If we review our day with the angels before we sleep, the process of resolving our worries works more efficiently. Dream time becomes more creative, brilliant ideas come to us, and dreams are more pleasant. (Some people actually do their best thinking in their sleep!)

Reserve some time before you go to sleep for a review of your day. Go over what worked and what didn't. If you are still holding onto worries and disappointments from the day, ask the angels to release them for you. Ask the angels for the chance to work things out in your dreams creatively. After you've gone through the gravity checklist—that is, your seriousness review of the day—switch your focus to the positive and give thanks for the blessings in your life. Think of things that happened during the day that were humorous and meaningful. Ask the angels to keep you in a sweet and light state when you fall asleep. Ask them to keep your dreams sweet and peaceful—taking you with them to the plane of heaven.

If you are worried about the upcoming day, try this technique: Take a piece of paper and write about the upcoming day as if it had already happened. For example: "This morning I woke up fresh and alert at 7:00 A.M., which gave me plenty of time to enjoy my morning coffee and think peacefully about my life. At 9:00 A.M., I left the house; the traffic was smooth, with every car in synch. I found the perfect parking place, and I even got to work early. At 10:00 A.M., my meeting with _____ went perfectly, and she agreed to _____. During lunch, I had more than enough time to take care of some errands, to eat, and to socialize. The rest of the day was very productive and creative. My drive home was wonderful, and dinner with _____ was incredibly romantic and sweet. . . . "

I hope you get the idea. When your script is done, ask the angels to bless it. Then, at the end of the "perfect" day, go over your list and see how well you did. This is a good technique to use when you have an important day coming up and you want some unseen help with it.

A similar technique involves visualizing the next day in your mind. As you do this, ask the angels for insight into the people you'll be seeing. What are they really like? Is there a common ground between you? What are their deepest desires? Ask the angels what phone calls you need to make, and how you can manage and remember the big and little details that so often elude us and end up causing us more work in the long run.

When you try this technique, think of yourself having a meeting with your invisible secretary (your copilot angel) and discuss ways your copilot can help you with the day ahead. This technique works! It works because you have loaded your unconscious mind with a program to follow. Our unconscious mind can follow time schedules quite well. Think of a home office that exists in your mind, taking care of the little details while you are out promoting yourself in the world.

Many people watch the news or a violent and stressful show on television right before going to sleep. News is rarely edifying and usually leaves us with a feeling of fear and discomfort, as does a show with violent images and messages. This is not a good way to fall asleep. Reading something inspiring or listening to relaxing music are good alternatives to the violence and degradation of late-night television. If you must watch T.V. before you go to bed, at least pick something humorous and light—if you can find it.

At bedtime, clear your mind and gather the angels around you, so that you can go to sleep in a higher state of consciousness. When you are no longer worried about the day you had and you've planned the upcoming day, cultivate a time of peaceful silence and fall asleep. Imagine the angels putting you to sleep, covering you with a warm, cozy blanket of golden love light, and flying around you all night, keeping away the monsters and ghosts and sprinkling gold dust on your hopes and dreams.

SUMMARY

Method

Bedtime angel review. Ask the angels to purify the atmosphere while you sleep, to bring you sweet dreams, and to help you bless the coming day.

Angels who can help

Call on your guardian angel and any other angels who will aid you in sleeping in peaceful bliss. The worry extinguishers, co-pilots, and brain program editors can help you sort out the day and plan the day ahead.

Tools and ideas

1. Review the day. What worked and what didn't? Go through a gravity checklist in your mind, releasing the heavy burdens you've accumulated. Call in the angels for insight and peace. Be thankful for the humorous and meaningful experiences you had during the day.
2. If you have a big day scheduled tomorrow and you are a bit worried about getting through it, try the technique of writing about exactly how you want everything in the next day to go as if it had already happened, as if you were entering it into your diary the following night. Then ask the angels to bless it, and to bring you insight in your dreams.
3. Manifest and visualize the next day in your mind. Meet the people, make the calls, and send the letters in your imagination, and then ask the angels to give you heavenly insight into what you will accomplish.
4. Find something edifying and inspiring to do or read before you fall asleep. Or just listen to relaxing music or watch something humorous and light on T.V.
5. Read about brain program editors in Chapter 8 for more assistance in eliminating the negatives.
6. Sweet dreams!

Chapter 21

Listening to Your Inner Guidance

Most of us never stop to give ourselves a quiet moment; we rush through our days and never process the information we absorb. We ignore ourselves with the hope that we won't have to "face the music" anytime soon. Facing the music is a lot easier when the angels play it for us. By meditating, centering ourselves, and praying, we can plug ourselves into the heaven circuit and process our information for the highest good.

There are a variety of approaches to meditation, such as focusing on a mantra, on imagery, or on physical objects, or simply paying attention to one's breathing. You may already be familiar with meditation and practice it regularly. Being centered comes from meditating and from taking the time to breathe and process information as it comes up, in a nonattached manner. Praying is a way of expressing our longing for insight and peace from the realm of heaven.

Angel Meditation

Start by finding a quiet and comfortable place to sit. Close your eyes and just be. Try not to think; if thoughts come to you, allow them in and then release them and go back to not thinking. *Pay attention to attention.* Never let attention become an effort, or try to force thoughts away. Don't let thoughts disturb you; just let them come and go. Now let your attention focus on angels. At this point, you may want to use the word *angel* as a form of mantra. Allow the word to take you wherever it will. Let a smile come over you, and notice the feeling of peace that comes with it. As you smile, feel yourself lifted and surrounded by white light. Ask the angels to lift you into heaven so that you can meet them. Ask to be an angel for a moment, and experience the lightness and happiness of the angels' realm. Get to know your guardian angel as you would a friend. Do this in whatever manner comes to you; there are no set rules. Ask the angels to guide you with their inspiring wisdom, and listen quietly for any messages they have for you. The messages may not come to you in words; often angels speak to you with feelings and images. Sometimes, the benefits of meditation come to the surface hours later. It may be that an idea was planted into your subconscious for use at a later time. During meditation, the angels sometimes spread out the pieces of your life, like the pieces of a puzzle, so that you can see what you have to work with. As you go through each day, another piece will fit into place, bringing you closer to the whole. (Then you can start another puzzle!)

When you are just getting to know angels, meditation may be a time for clearing out negative belief systems and emotional blocks that keep you from connecting with the heavenly realm. (See Chapter 19 on declarations to the angels.) Be patient, and do the work. Purify your consciousness of whatever is limiting you. Eventually, your inner wisdom will come through loud and clear, and the light and happiness of the angels will stay with you throughout the day.

Angel Centering

Being centered means your spirit is in alignment with your body. It means there is a balance: your head is not totally in the clouds in an avoidance of life, but neither are you completely grounded to the earth and overreacting to life situations. Centering is a way of synchronizing our energy. If our energy is scattered, we are going in different directions within ourselves; we are going in circles, so to speak. If we synchronize our energy, we can head in one direction and accomplish our goals. Centering synchronizes our energy with our higher self and with the angels who guide us.

Centering harmonizes our body/mind. When we are centered, we cannot be knocked off balance or fall over easily. We are able to accept the reality of our situations and to use our inner resources and creativity to deal with that reality. Sometimes, just a change of scenery will center you—for example, going outside for a breath of fresh air, or admiring a beautiful garden. Exercise and movement can center you—for example, taking a long walk on the beach, or dancing to your favorite song. Playing a musical instrument, painting, cooking, and writing (especially in a journal) are ways to find your center by paying attention to the activity, and thinking of nothing else.

Centering yourself is a good habit and talent to develop. Meditating is one way of centering yourself. During the course of the day, however, you may not have time to do a full meditation. Taking a time-out is like doing a quick meditation. If you feel yourself getting off balance, take a time-out. Find a place where you can close your eyes and calm your breathing. Clear your mind and ask for immediate angel guidance and insight into what knocked you off balance. Now, bring a smile to your being and relax. When you are centering yourself, ask the angels for creativity and peace and then accept it and go back to what you are doing with a refreshed attitude.

Get in the habit of not overreacting to situations; get away from the "everything is either good or bad" syndrome. Adopt the perspective of: "This is interesting; let me stop and center myself for a moment so I don't freak out." Step back and observe the situation from an objective position. Realign your spirit with your body/mind. Pull yourself together by taking a time-out with the angels.

Praying

Prayer is our chance to talk to the higher power in our lives, whether we think of it as God, the angels, Buddha, a saint, a bodhisattva, or simply the Universe. Prayer is something we can do alone or with others. You can pray by singing or writing a poem. You may experience prayer as a peak experience when you are giving thanks and blessings. Sometimes, we pray and don't even realize it—for example, when we're feeling down and we cry out for release.

F. Forrester Church talks about three kinds of prayer in his book *Entertaining Angels: A Guide to Heaven*. The first kind of prayer is confession, through which we make peace with the enemy within us. The second kind of prayer links self to others; this happens when we ask for blessings for others and for situations we want. The third kind of prayer involves saying "yes" to life and giving ourselves over to God; this is how we express gratitude and trust in the universe.

Prayer is personal: We all have our own ways or praying, but basically prayer involves expressing ourselves verbally to God. We can be specific in our prayers, relaying exactly what we want, or we can ask for blessings from God's abundance and trust that everything will work out. Prayer can center us and guide us back on track. Prayer is the way we talk to angels, and by meditating we listen to their response. Prayer is asking for divine intercession, both for ourselves and others.

When you pray to the angels, pray as if "it is already done"; in other words, thank the angels in advance for taking care of your burdens. Pray that it will be done on earth as it is in heaven, for the highest good of all concerned. When you pray to the angels, remember that they work for a higher power (meaning God or whatever term you use to describe the highest spiritual force in your life). So always thank God and the angels in your prayers, and ask that you be blessed with peace.

Creating an Altar

An altar is a space of spiritual focus. Altars in churches are tables on which offerings are made to God, such as the bread and wine of communion. You may already have an altar or shrine in your home; a lot of people do these days. If you don't, you may want to create one so that you can have a place of spiritual focus. Gather small objects that are sacred to you, such as pictures, statues, a vase for flowers, prayer beads, crystals, rocks, shells, plaques, icons, an incense burner—whatever feels right to you. Now, find an empty space to create your altar. A small table, an area in a bookcase, the top of a dresser, or a windowsill can all work well. If you are uncomfortable about having people see your altar, find a subtle place in your room. You can make your altar so simple that no one will even notice it It helps to have a beautiful cloth to add inspiring colors. Always make room for a candle. Angels love candlelight. Candlelight illuminates and purifies the atmosphere and attracts angels.

After you have created your altar or shrine, light the candle and sit quietly in front of it. Draw in the beauty and ask the angels to join you. Put on some inspiring and peaceful music—harps and flutes attract angels. Burn some incense if you like. Let yourself find joy, love, and divine humor in your spiritual contemplation, and inhale the golden light you've created.

SUMMARY

Method
Meditating, centering, and creating a space for spiritual focus

as a way of attracting and getting to know angels.

Angels who can help

Call on the angels to join you in your meditations.

Tools and ideas

1. Do an angel meditation as a way of connecting with the heaven plane.
2. Learn to take time-outs during the day to center yourself and connect with the angels for inspiration. Center yourself whenever you feel the urge to overreact to or to label any situation as good or bad.
3. Pray. Verbally express your longing for peace and communion with the angels.
4. Create a shrine or altar as a place for spiritual focus and centering.
5. Connect yourself to the spiritual beauty in life with flowers, music, and candlelight—the elements that attract angels.

Chapter 22

Noticing Angels in Everyday Life

It's fun to notice the way angels are sung about, portrayed in art, and talked about in our everyday life. By everyday life I mean the routines in our lives involving external reality—for example, listening to the radio, watching T.V., going places each day in our cars, noticing people on the street. When we become aware of angels, it is fun to notice how often we hear the word *angel* each day, and how often we see angels in art and even in people.

Most of us leave the house at least once a day. And most of us listen to a recording or to music on the radio in our home or car. Most stores and restaurants have music playing. Start noticing how often you hear the word *angel* in the songs you hear. Go through some of your old records and notice how many times you come across titles with the word *angel* in them.

When you go to the grocery store or pharmacy, start noticing all the products that use the word *angel* in their name. They range from toilet paper and perfume to pasta and liqueur. One time, my friend and I decided to have an angel food dinner, with

113

angel hair pasta as the main dish and angel food cake for dessert; we added other appropriate items to go with the theme. Many products have heaven or paradise as their theme, or use the names of specific angels on the labels. Celestial themes are also popular.

When you see paintings and statues, look for angels. You might walk by them all the time and not even notice. You will see angels in magazines and on book covers. It is fun to see how contemporary artists portray angels. The New Age visionary artists have created especially beautiful paintings of angels. There are greeting cards with angels pictured on them for all seasons and occasions. Museums flourish with angel statues and paintings.

You can also find angels on television. There is even a primetime show about an angel who comes to earth as a human to help people. Movies about angels, both new and old, often make their way to our T.V. sets. Occasionally, you can hear about an angel of the moment on the evening news or on a T.V. magazine show. An angel of the moment is a human who is a rescuer. Whether these angels rescue people from danger or from the darkness, either way they are inspiring to hear about and deserve more time on the air. Also, if you are watching a news story about a disaster in which miraculously only a few people were hurt be assured that there was unseen help from heaven.

Visualizing angels in the clouds is fun. Sometimes, angels show up in reflections on glass or water. I have taken pictures of strange blobs of light that appeared for no reason and that looked to me like angels. One time I took a picture of two friends of mine sitting at a table, in what I thought was the same light, but one of them came out so overexposed in the photograph that I could hardly see her image. This didn't really surprise me, though, because this friend is full of light and very much like an angel. Stains on old buildings, paint splatters, rock formations, and strange lights in the sky—all can hold the visual image of angels.

Increasing your awareness of angels in everyday life will help you formulate your own concepts about who they are and how they can help you. If you become highly interested in angels, you will want to read more about them. Several books about angels are listed in Part Five, along with other sources of information that will increase your knowledge and understanding of angels.

Chapter 23

Recognizing Signs of Angels' Play

An angel's work is actually play. When you want to attract angels into your life, you must recognize the signs of play that mean they are with you. Recognizing and acknowledging angels is important for keeping your relationship with them alive and prominent in your life.

One meaning of play is "free movement." Play does not restrict or control anyone. Play is also a means for interspecies communication—for example, humans and dolphins play together, and dogs, cats, and humans play together. Another example of interspecies communication through play is between angels and humans.

Synchronicity is one way the angels play with us. For a detailed description of synchronicity, read about synchronism agents in Chapter 6. Basically, a synchronism is a coincidental event that seems to take on a meaning beyond the obvious. When angels are playing with us, they communicate by arranging coincidences and favorable meetings.

Another way angels play with us is by providing humor at our most serious moments. They may arrange for something hysterically funny to occur just when you can't take it anymore.

Unexplainable feelings of peace and well-being mean that angels are at play around you. Visualize them playing all around you, scaring off the negative thoughts and worrisome situations that interfere with your peace of mind. Visualize them catching the negatives and turning them into positives before they get to you.

Good luck and good fortune are fun games the angels play with us. Luck seems to be a gift from the universe, but actually we create our own good luck by believing we deserve it. When we believe and know we deserve good luck and fortune, the angels help it along. The reason luck is a game is that it involves a certain kind of work on our part to play it. As with playing any game, there are opportunities we must grab and actions we must take to win. The angels help us understand just what luck is all about.

Hope is present when angels are around. There is always hope. Hope is a seed the angels plant in our consciousness; then they water and fertilize it to grow and flourish in our lives. Hope and faith can heal physical and mental maladies. They give us the will to find the way.

Playing with the angels can give us the feeling that we are so light we might just float away. The lightness is so prominent that we may even forget we have bodies. Experiencing this light is pure joy. It is a peak experience of love. It is a gift the angels give us to let us know they are near and that we deserve to feel good.

Understanding and recognizing the signs that mean angels are at play in our lives will help us prolong the positive feelings and bring us a deeper and closer connection with them. Each time you ask the angels to help you with something, look for clues of their play. Then thank them, and tell them to keep up the good play.

Chapter 24

Wearing Clothes
Angels Like

One way to attract angels is to wear the kinds of clothes they like. By now, you probably have a sense of the qualities of the angels that surround you. Wearing something that the angels will like is a personal choice based on your own perception and idea of angels. Here are some ideas I've found in the books I've read on angels and from talking with people about angels.

COLORS TO WEAR TO ATTRACT SPECIFIC ANGELS

>Guardians: rose or pink (an aura of divine affection), and
>   soft green
>Healing angels: deep sapphire blue
>Angels of birth: sky blue
>Ceremonial and music angels: white
>Nature angels: apple green
>Angels of art and wisdom: yellow

The seraphim (the "burning ones" are the first choir of
   angels, and are the closest to God's throne): crimson red
The cherubim (the next choir): blue
Archangel Michael: deep green, vivid blue, gold, and rose
Archangel Raphael: pale blue and soft greens
Archangel Gabriel: tans, browns, and dark greens

COLORS TO WEAR TO ATTRACT MOST ANGELS

Study the colors of an abalone shell (mother-of-pearl) and select
clothing in various combinations of these colors. These beautiful
light pastel colors will make you feel light and heavenly. When
you feel this way, you will surely attract angels.

TYPES OF CLOTHING TO WEAR

Clothes that flow and drape your body
Breezy clothes that catch the wind and make you feel a part
   of nature
Clown suits that make others laugh
Angel costumes with wings and halos
Clothes that make you feel and look good
All-white clothing that helps you reflect light around you

FLOWER FRAGRANCES THAT ATTRACT ANGELS

Jasmine and rose are said to be noticeable when angels (especially
guardian angels) are near. Pine is said to attract healing angels,
and its scent is noticeable when they are near. Sandalwood is
the fragrance that the creativity ministers or muses are supposed
to like.

   Assign fragrances to the angels you want near you, and bring
flowers into your home, burn incense, or wear perfume with
these fragrances. For example:

Honeysuckle: the messengers
Gardenia: worry extinguishers and prosperity brokers

Hyacinth: soul angels
Lilac: happiness trainers

OTHER IDEAS

When you are in a difficult situation, imagine yourself wearing a halo and surround yourself with white light. Imagine your car wearing a field of white light to protect you on the road. Imagine your house wearing an aura of white light to protect you from negative forces.

Wearing something angels like is all in fun. It works because angels like to participate in fun. It is your own game and your own rules. So use your intuition. If you feel strongly about a certain color or fragrance for attracting specific angels, bring the color or fragrance into your life and the angels will be near.

Part Four

Living an
Angelic Life

About Part Four:
An Angelic Life-Style

Part Four is about living an angelic life-style. This doesn't mean that all of a sudden you are a perfect little angel in all you do; it has nothing to do with perfection. Perfection is boring, and the angels know this. Living an angelic life only means that you have chosen to incorporate lightness into whatever you do. To bring lightness into your life, you may need to make more room for it. By bringing in lightness, you bring in angels, so it is impossible to have one without the other. Part Four discusses ways to make room in your life for lightness and angels.

Chapter 25 is about forgiving yourself and others as a means of releasing the past. Forgiveness equals release. By practicing forgiveness, you open up many channels to lightness.

Chapter 26 explores the difference between empathy and sympathy. Chances are good that you are a very sensitive being who can fall into periods of heaviness if those around you are in pain. We can't ignore our friends when they are in pain, and we would not want to be ignored ourselves. It helps to know some techniques for dealing with other people's pains and problems without going down yourself. In fact, by remaining light you will be able to help them more.

But helping others requires remaining light in a responsible way. Chapter 27, on the consequences of light behavior, tells you about the balance to strive for when you've adopted the philosophy of lightness.

Chapter 28 looks at enlightenment in connection with angels, as another way to incorporate lightness into your spiritual path.

Random angel testing is a game the angels play with humans and is described in Chapter 29. This game has the objective of lightening up and waking up the participants.

The angel health and beauty program in Chapter 30 lists ways you can lighten up physically, leaving room for even more lightness in your life.

Chapters 31 and 32 address issues that get in the way of lightness, which are not very fun at all. The topics discussed need to be looked at for insight into how and why we humans experience the "downs" in the "ups and downs" of life. Ideally, the more we learn about the down side, the easier it will be to stay away from it and incorporate more levels of light—more "ups"— into our life-style.

The information in Part Four is compatible with the methods in Part Three and will help you expand and personalize these methods. Also, as you read Part Four, consider which of the angels described in Part Two can help you lead a more angelic life.

Welcome to the life-styles of the light and angelic!

Chapter 25

Practicing Forgiveness and Release

Look at the humans on this planet as either extending love or as fearful and sending out a call for love.

Gerald Jampolsky

Forgiveness means ceasing to feel anger and resentment toward others about offenses you feel they have committed. The act of forgiving releases you from resentment and anger so that these negative emotions don't consume you. True forgiveness is a difficult lesson if we are convinced that others have harmed us purposely. We want them to ask us for forgiveness, but they may not agree with our perception of the situation. Whether or not a negative action was purposely directed at us doesn't matter. Facts surrounding the situation don't really matter either (unless you are in court); it is how we perceive the situation and how it makes us feel that causes trouble. The pain, anger, and resentment that is stored in our consciousness when we won't forgive and release can cause big trouble in our lives.

Current research is finding a link between unexpressed anger and resentment and a tendency to get cancer and other illnesses. Anger and resentment chip away at our happiness and cloud the present. It is difficult to be happy when our minds are stuck on past situations that have caused us pain. Practicing forgiveness releases us from the limitations of the past, clears up the negatives, and gives us a clean slate for the present.

Sometimes, the people we love the most are the hardest to forgive. If there are some people who you find especially unforgivable, write a note of forgiveness to their highest angels. The problem may be that you don't know *how* to forgive them. Cultivate a willingness to release the situation. Write or speak to their highest angels and let it be known that you are willing to forgive and forget and go on with your happiness. Imagine your highest angel talking to the other person's highest angel and working out the differences between you, ending in peace and laughter. Willingness is the key ingredient on your part; let the angels take care of the rest.

According to Emmet Fox, "When you hold resentment against anyone, you are bound to that person by a cosmic link, a real though mental chain. You are tied by a cosmic tie to the thing you hate. The one person perhaps in the whole world whom you most dislike is the very one to whom you are attaching yourself by a hook that is stronger than steel." Resentment and anger can have a snowball effect in your mind. Just as a snowball picks up more snow as it rolls down a hill, anger picks up more fuel as it grows in your mind, picking up misperceptions. In other words, if a small offense is not taken care of and released immediately, it can grow into a huge offense in your mind, one which will be difficult to forgive later.

Abraham Lincoln was once criticized for the manner in which he dealt with his "enemies." He answered the criticism by saying, "Do I not destroy my enemies when I make them my friends?" At some point in your life, you may have been told, that you must love your enemies. This is a lot easier said than done, especially if *we* are our own worst enemy. When the enemy is ourselves, we are usually the last to know because we can't step outside ourselves with total objectivity to see the attacks we wage on ourselves.

One day I was driving my car and I kept noticing things that were wrong with all the other cars on the road. One had a taillight out, one was spewing dark smoke out of its tailpipe, and another had a bad tire. Then I realized that if any of these things were wrong with my car, I wouldn't know it because I was busy driving. I, too, could have a taillight out or a bad exhaust system, and not even know about it. Unless I were to stop the car, get out, and watch the car in action, I would not really know what is going on with it. Well, how can we get out of our lives and really notice all the things we need to fix? We can't exactly get out and walk around, but we can become more aware of the ways in which we sabotage ourselves and act as our own worst enemy.

The key is to adopt a pattern of awareness so that we can detect and change negative thoughts directed toward ourselves. Learning to forgive *ourselves* is extremely important. When it comes to forgiveness, we are hardest on ourselves. If guilt is keeping you from forgiving yourself, then work on releasing guilt first. Guilt consists of unexpressed resentment and fear or anticipation of punishment or a harsh reaction from others. If a situation with someone is making you feel guilty, this could mean that you actually feel that that person is trying to control or sway you into doing something you don't want to do. This breeds resentment. We resent it when our time is wasted, but most of us do things for others because we believe we "should." Situations involving "shoulds" or trying to live down to another's expectations breed resentment, resentment breeds guilt, guilt looks for a way to punish, and punishment means pain.

Guilt can also surface when we feel "too good." You may have a brain program that tells you you don't deserve to feel good: "How dare you feel good when others feel bad?" You may feel guilty for having so much when others have so little. You imagine them disapproving of and envying your happiness. Forgiveness is an act of unconditional love. This means we must love ourselves unconditionally and treat ourselves well. Ultimately, guilt has the same effect as unexpressed anger and resentment; you can literally make yourself sick with guilt.

The bottom line is that you won't be as happy as you deserve to be if guilt and hatred are taking up space in your consciousness. Whatever the hate results from, get rid of it; don't punish yourself needlessly. Ask the angels for release and be willing to let the hatred go. Call on your cheerleaders. They like you no matter what. Their main cheer is: "Don't give up; we like who you are. We are proud of who you are!" Cheer with them and learn how to love yourself unconditionally regardless of any stupid mistakes you have made in the past. We all have the right to make asses out of ourselves as long as we can have a good laugh about how funny we are. So lighten up and don't be so hard on yourself!

Make a list of the things you have done for which you want forgiveness. Think of the things you have done that may be keeping you from unconditional happiness. Declare formally that you are forgiving yourself for the situations listed. Ask your guardian angel to help you release the situations and take care of the how, while you concentrate on being willing to release your list. Here is a sample list.

I formally and willingly forgive myself for the following situations:

1. Complaining
2. Forgetting to count my blessings
3. Listening to and internalizing criticism
4. Forgetting that at any time I can change my perception and see other humans and myself as innocent
5. Blaming
6. Feeling guilty
7. Getting angry

8. Being conditional
9. Worrying
10. Feeling envy, jealousy, and greed
11. Overeating and jeopardizing my health
12. Being in denial
13. Losing faith and not following through
14. Harboring negative brain programs
15. Forgetting to call in the angels when needed

After you have made your list, try to see how funny and endearing you are. Love your humanness. If there are people you find difficult to forgive, make a list of their offenses and then release them, and remember to check out the humor in their lists. Always ask the angels to help you release your lists and transmute the energy.

Practicing forgiveness brings you closer to happiness without reason. It frees you from the past. It allows freedom in the present. It takes away limits, and so frees the future. Forgiveness allows us to be happy in the now without guilt, anger, and resentment causing us pain. Forgiving yourself and others without condition is the key to releasing the past and healing the present. Forgiveness is an act of love. As Louis Gittner says, "Love can build highways out of dead ends."

PRACTICE IDEAS

1. If there are people or loved ones you are finding difficult to forgive, then write a letter of forgiveness to their highest angels.
2. If there are people you need to forgive, visualize meeting with these people or their highest angels to clear the air.
3. If you are being hard on yourself for one reason or another, write down a forgiveness list as described above, and hand it over to the angels.
4. Adopt a pattern to detect and intercept negative thoughts directed toward yourselves and others; then transmute the thoughts or throw them out.

5. If you are your own worst enemy, make friends with yourself. If there are too many "shoulds" and feelings of guilt in your daily life, this is a sign that you need to forgive yourself for not being "perfect" and to incorporate the angels into your life. This is also a sign that you need to play and have fun. Attain a feeling of lightness toward yourself by calling on the angels or by writing a formal statement to them regarding your forgiveness of yourself. Read and internalize any information you find about loving yourself and raising your level of self-esteem.

The following Loving Kindness Meditation, from the tradition of Theravada Buddhism, is quoted from Rick Fields's *Chop Wood, Carry Water.*

If anyone has hurt me or harmed me knowingly or unknowingly in thought, word, or deed, I freely forgive them.

And I too ask forgiveness if I have hurt anyone or harmed anyone knowingly or unknowingly in thought, word, or deed.

May I be happy
May I be peaceful
May I be free

May my friends be happy
May my friends be peaceful
May my friends be free

May my enemies be happy
May my enemies be peaceful
May my enemies be free

May all beings be happy
May all beings be peaceful
May all beings be free

Chapter 26

Empathy Versus Sympathy

There is a fine line between empathy and sympathy. Empathy is understanding another person's feelings without getting caught up in the feelings. When we have sympathy for others, we connect with their pain and we suffer if they are suffering. If we have empathy for others, we can remain happy even if they are sad, and we can still help them by understanding and recognizing their pain without feeling it ourselves. Remaining happy and light as long as we are not pushy and forceful will help others lighten up in due time.

Sympathy includes an element of pity or feeling sorry for someone. Pitying others is not helpful; it is condescending. Sympathizing with others can have the effect of continuing a downward process. It is like a man coming by on a sled that is heading downhill for diaster and stopping to pick you up. If you get on, you go down with him. If you turn him around or stop him by helping him recognize the end result, you help him.

Empathy conveys a message of equality and strengthens self-esteem. You are not putting yourself above others and saying, "Let me help you." Nor are you lowering yourself and feeling bad, too. Empathizing means you are allowing a person to be and to explore. You will be there as a caring and unconditional listener. Unconditional listening is a rare and delicate art. Listening with an open heart and mind without expectations, projections, emotional investment, or judgments is difficult to master. The angels can help.

Are you someone people come to with problems and sorrows? Are you someone others seek out to talk to about themselves in general? If you are, consider it a high compliment. It means you are trusted. Learning how to listen without it damaging or interfering with your own psyche is important. It is also good to know the way angels can help you help someone else.

First of all, ask the angels to protect you from reacting emotionally to someone else's problems. This means you must stay centered within yourself when you are listening to others talk about their lives and their perceptions. Practice listening to people without thinking things like "that's good . . . that's bad . . . you should . . . he should . . . she should not . . . do . . . don't"—in essence, try to free your mind from judgments of any kind. See the situation as it exists by itself; free it from your projections as much as possible. Try not to "react and relate" to information that involves people, regardless of how much you care about them. Don't take sides if someone is talking about a relationship. If you take sides even in concept, you will soon find yourself sinking into identification with one person or the other and becoming emotionally involved in the discord, thus amplifying the problem of the person you are trying to assist, and reinforcing the bad feeling between the two people.

Here is one technique that will make it easier to hear people fully while avoiding the trap of becoming emotionally involved in their conflict: When you listen to somebody talking, listen for what they are really saying. Repeat key phrases back to them. For example, if a friend says, "＿＿＿ really made me angry today because he went somewhere without me and he knows I wanted to go with him," repeat back to her, "You are really angry

because you wanted to go to _____ and _____ didn't take you."
Then she will know you are listening to her, and she'll go a step
further: "He always does this to me, and I'm afraid he doesn't
want to be with me anymore." Repeat back, "You are afraid
_____ is going his own way without you." You have gotten even
more information, and you now know that your friend is dealing
with the fear of potential rejection. By repeating information
back to other people, you allow them to direct the conversation
to the areas where the real issues lie.

When it seems to be the right time, you can confront people
about the real issues that are upsetting them. Remember that the
feelings are real, that they are experiencing pain, and that it
doesn't matter whether you or anyone else agrees with them.
The facts do not matter; the only thing that matters is *how* and
why the situation is causing them pain. Of course, no one is
expecting you to be a professional counselor, but it never hurts
to learn and practice ways of listening to others that let them
know they are heard and cared for—and to do this without
involving yourself in the pain. In this way, you are practicing
empathy for others and leaving sympathy out.

If people are talking on and on about the behavior of others
in their lives, notice how often they are actually describing themselves. If you feel compelled to point this out to them, do it in
a loving way.

The angels can help you in a variety of ways. When you are
with people you care about who are having a rough time, ask the
angels to surround the room in the white-pink-gold light of healing and love. Ask your guardian angel to confer with the other
people's guardians to give you insight into their pain and suffering
and to guide you in the best ways of helping them. Ask that the angels and your guardian keep you centered and free from identify-
ing with pain that is not yours. Ask the other people's guardians
to let them know that you can be trusted, that you will be unconditional, and that you will not judge or react—that you will just
listen. Ask your own guardian to help you be this way.

Your overall objective will be to bring in humor at some point—to "leave them laughing," so to speak. Do this with the utmost delicacy and ask the angels to help you; it is one of their specialties. Ask the guardians of both you and the other people for the release of laughter every once in a while. Laughter will help you clarify the issues. Laughter will free both you and those you are helping for creative problem solving. Laughter is a good way to introduce "angel help" to others if they aren't already aware of its existence.

When the people see the light and lighten up, they will be receptive to angels. Think of any of the methods in Part Three that could help these people. Think of any angel stories you could tell them. Then let them know that they have a guardian angel and that this guardian angel is around to protect them and lead them to a happier way of being. Encourage them to try a few methods together with you, such as writing to the guardians of people who have hurt them and writing some declarations to the angels stating positive changes they want to make in their lives. Ask that the angels bless all of you with healing and light.

When all is said and done, think of how much you learn from listening to others. Examine any tension you feel is clinging to you from time you've spent with others and their problems. Write about it in your angel journal or just meditate on it. Somehow, let yourself process the information you absorb. Know that you can protect your center and remain happy when others are sad. Know the difference between empathy and sympathy. Know that you can help others by simply listening unconditionally to them. Know that the angels can help you achieve all of the above.

Chapter 27

The Consequences
of Light Behavior

Enlighten up!

Steve Bucher

Taking yourself lightly and behaving in a lighthearted way has a favorable effect on all aspects of your life. Lightheated people would never want to offend or hurt others with their behavior, so it is important to examine just what is meant by taking yourself lightly and almost nothing seriously.

First of all, why is it that angels want us to become more like them by taking ourselves lightly? This is mainly a matter of trust. As humans, we have basic survival issues to face on a daily basis. We have to make sure we have water to drink, food to eat, and shelter and safety to protect us. For some people, these needs are taken care of without a worry; most of us work for money to pay for these basics. With working comes a certain amount of stress and worry—worry about having enough to get by and still having time for some fun and creativity. The way angels see it, if we can trust and have faith in them and the laws of an abundant universe, we will be taken care of without all the worry. In turn, we won't have to take these survival issues so seriously, we can have more fun in life, and our work can be play.

Angels provide protection in the form of a personal guardian who is always by your side. They provide food and shelter by sending messages through your higher self, guiding you in the direction of the right career and opportunities. Of course, they will only do this for you if you want them to—so somehow you or your higher self has to ask them. The only thing angels can't do is live your life for you. Angels want to help us with the serious issues we face each day so that we can be lighter and more creative—and in turn more fun to be around.

Angels want to remove from our lives the solemnity and pessimism that result from reacting to too many things in a serious manner and creating a heavier gravity field around ourselves. This doesn't mean that if your children come to you hurt you can't take them seriously or that if someone is truly asking for your help or empathy that you can't respond to their request. (See Chapter 26 on empathy versus sympathy and basic listening techniques.) It means take your loved ones to heart (a light heart) but not with gravity.

When those we love come to us hurt or in serious trouble, we can keep a light heart and still help them know that we love and care for them. If we need to discuss a "serious" issue with someone, we can still be happy and optimistic. The angels will help you balance lightness in your life so that no one is hurt by your behavior (unless someone wants to be hurt by you). The angels want to see loving lightness in humans—*not* carelessness. Be carefree, not careless.

When people are in serious and solemn moods, they may be offended if you treat their problems and perceptions too lightly. Developing the right balance of lightness in relation to other humans is important. Have you ever been in a bad mood and had to be around a cheerful person? In a state of depression, being around a cheerful and light person can make people angry. One time I was sincerely angry at someone because of her behavior in a certain situation. All I wanted was someone to listen to me while I aired my anger. The person I chose kept saying, "Oh, what a silly girl. She is so silly. That is so silly." Well, of course it was silly—everything is silly—but I did not want to hear that at the time and it made me even angrier. I learned several valuable things about myself from this experience. Later I realized that I have probably done the same thing over and over to this same person and to most of my friends. While trying to make people see the humor (the light), I wasn't listening in the most caring and unconditional way that I could.

It is wise to adjust our lightness and cheerfulness to the right level around people who are having a hard time if we want to be true friends. Listen unconditionally and wait for the right moment; wait for a cue from them before you begin trying to cheer them up. This way, they can ease out of their pain and join in your happiness on their own. In other words, we wouldn't want to force-feed lightness to anyone.

Laughter is important for lightening up any situation. Just be sure you are not "laughing in someone's face." Find a way to get others laughing with you in serious situations; it is a great release. Call on the humor transformers if you are in need of laughter. In any crisis I've experienced, I have noticed that at some point the people involved needed a good laugh, and it happened naturally. Even at funerals, people find a release by laughing. This doesn't mean disrespect for those who are deceased; it's actually a good indication that they are greatly loved and appreciated.

When I hear myself say (or think), "This is a very serious matter," I instantly get the urge to laugh. When I am forced to go out and take care of "serious matters" and I run into people who are way too serious, once again I get an urge to laugh. This seems so funny to me, and they usually look funny too. A fun thing to do is to try to get a smile or laugh out of people when they are caught in the trap of seriousness. This takes some skill, but it can be done by anyone willing to try. Of course, always do this with a sense of love, never out of anger or as a punishment. First, try smiling yourself. As you smile, imagine light radiating from your being to reach out and zap the people. If this doesn't work, you can try telling a joke. If they get more serious after the joke, you may be in too deep and need to stop. If people have chosen to work with the public, I think they have a certain responsibility to be pleasant. This is just my opinion, but when we are out among others of our species an air of kindness and hospitality creates a pattern of magic in the universe—a pattern that attracts the angels.

When you go out in the world with a light heart, you want the consequences of your light behavior to be positive. It is not wise to lecture or preach! If people are feeling heavy, depressed, or even paranoid, there's nothing worse than laying your own belief system on them, as if agreeing with your doctrine or view of the world would help them. This can be especially bad if you come on with the self-righteous attitude of many people who attribute their own success or happiness to some belief they hold or some code of conduct they practice. People can become "belief dependent," and they are usually off base as far as their own explanation of their success goes. They become superstitious. It's easy to make other people feel bad, even worse than they were already feeling, by convincing them that the problem is their failure or inability to believe as you do. Well, now I'm lecturing and preaching! How does it make you feel? It's so difficult to be perfect, isn't it? So we might as well have a good laugh at ourselves and not take the process of belief so seriously.

KEYS TO RESPONSIBLE LIGHT BEHAVIOR

1. Angels want us to be less solemn and to worry less over the everyday survival issues we face, so that we are happier and

more creative. They remind us to give our burdens over to a higher power and to trust in the protection they provide.

2. We must do a lightness check to make sure that we are not taking things that require our loving attention too lightly. Carefree behavior is fine as long as it is not careless.

3. The consequences of behaving lightly must be positive, or it is not true lightness. In other words, take life lightly in the spirit of love.

4. Laughter is a great release for serious occasions, as long as it is not totally inappropriate. Cues from others let us know when to introduce laughter.

5. Be wary of force-feeding lightness to others when they are not ready for it, or not in the mood.

6. Beware of the "belief system" mentality in yourself and others. Practice not preaching about what you practice!

7. Allow the dynamics of change to operate in your life. Change the rules when you feel stuck in a systematic practice.

Chapter 28

Angels and Enlightenment

Since everything is but an apparition,
perfect in being what it is,
having nothing to do with good or bad,
acceptance or rejection,
one may well burst out in laughter.

Long-Chen-Pa

Enlightenment is a state of being in light. To enlighten is to impart spiritual (intellectual) knowledge — to shed light on something essential. To be enlightened means to be free from prejudice and ignorance and to possess the spiritual knowledge that sheds light. From the above, we can surmise that enlightenment is the state of being completely in light, totally and spiritually informed, and free from having to judge and compare. The opposite of enlightenment is a state of mental darkness; the curtains are pulled so that the light won't get in.

According to most spiritual seekers, attaining enlightenment is the goal of life on earth. When we reach the state of enlightenment, we will know the answers to the questions of ontology (the metaphysical category that asks the question "What's it all about?") and teleology (the metaphysical category that asks the question "Why are we here?"). This boils down to: Who is directing this big picture, and do I really have a starring role or am I just an extra?

Angels are constantly in a state of light. They shed lightness and spiritually awaken us every chance they get. Angels send messages that tell us to cease comparing, judging, and emotionally reacting to the serious issues we face each day. In essence, angels are the epitome of enlightenment. And they live in the same neighborhood (heaven) as the creator of the universe.

Angels are the perfect teachers for us if we are seeking enlightenment. The catch is that according to the angels the experience of human life is ridiculous and absurd—and way too serious. By the angels' standards, once we really understand this, we will be enlightened. So what is the point of striving to attain a state if everything is seen as ridiculous? Well, one reason is that you will burst out laughing, because you will be one with the divine humor that permeates the universe.

We usually run into blocks on the path to enlightenment, because we forget to take along our sense of humor. Humor is definitely needed at all stages on the path of enlightenment. Angels can be of assistance by giving us a spiritual lightening up. Angels teach us that enlightenment releases us from the seriousness of life, and frees us from the traps of survival and emotional perceptions. All these traps occur first in our minds. Angels want to release us from these traps so that we can rest in the bliss of their realm.

When one connects completely with the angels (which only happens for brief previews if you haven't yet reached the state of chronic enlightenment), the peak experience of joy and bliss is indescribable. It is a moment of total freedom. The angels' message is: Give up and rest in God's love, and be one with the divine humor of the universe. The closer we come to a state of divine humor, the happier we will be. Any step we take freely toward enlightened humor will multiply our understanding of the ultimate question.

Enlightenment is the state in which you have merged completely with your higher self. Your higher self is able to have constant contact with angels in the realm of heaven. Just think of that—a chance to joke around with the angels whenever you want!

Enlightenment is hilarious, and life *is* absurd. We humans love a challenge and a game. Each time we get closer to being released from the human qualities that block enlightenment, something else comes up. For example, you finally get to a point where you aren't attached to the pain and suffering of others. You can be carefree, and you feel that you can go anywhere in the universe and survive with total freedom. Then you add a child to your life and everything changes. Now you have a whole new set of emotions and instincts to follow and integrate—as well as a new capacity for love.

Apparently, you will never run out of lessons to learn on this earth. But that is what makes human life fun and meaningful. If you attain enlightenment, you still have to go on living. The closer you get to enlightenment, the closer heaven gets to your reality of living on earth, so enlightenment is worth pursuing. Angels teach us to enlighten up! Loving humor makes everything seem a little easier to take and understand. Most of the lessons we have to learn on this earth are lessons that will increase our capacity for love. Love isn't heavy. Love is light; it is the highest angelic ideal.

Practice finding loving humor in all the things you do in the name of enlightenment. In each person you talk to, each book you read, each holy teacher you seek out, look for lightness and humor. If you miss it or find that it isn't there, go on to something else quick! Solemn spiritual rituals and the solemn people who practice them take enlightenment far too seriously.

Have you ever been involved in a serious religious ceremony and in the middle of it you got an urge to laugh hysterically?

Some churches and religious organizations seem to think that acting in a serious manner means respect for religion. Some religions take all the joy out of worship by demanding that people listen to a serious, solemn service talking about how bad humans are. This is supposed to lead us to "perfection"—but who wants it? Not I, and not the angels!

Angels are the ones who want to make us laugh during serious religious ceremonies. They are all over the place wanting to spread joy and humor. Their message is that we are loved unconditionally by God and the universe (and this love has nothing to do with being perfect). This message deserves lighthearted celebration and mirthful expression whenever it is heard. I would guess that there are more angels around people who are having fun and laughing, regardless of the circumstances, than in churches where people are being indoctrinated in seriousness.

Humor bypasses the need for strict and rigid spiritual practices. A day spent laughing will bring us closer to God than a day of heavy soul-searching. This is because laughter brings us closer to the real us—the lovable us, the happy us, the free us, the us others want to be around. Laughing frees our creativity so the soul-searching process unfolds in a natural, rather than a forced, manner. No need to push the river. Just build a raft, hop on it, and burst out laughing at the bends and rapids along the way.

Chapter 29

Random Angel Testing

*Do not forget or neglect to extend hospitality to strangers –
being friendly, cordial and gracious – for by this some have
entertained angels without knowing it.*

Hebrews 13:2

It may seem dangerous these days to acknowledge strangers in
any way, especially to be hospitable to them, but most of us have
developed a way of knowing intuitively when we are in danger.
If you know and believe that you are protected, being friendly
and helpful to strangers can be fun and quite enlightening. I'm
not suggesting that you do anything unintelligent, such as thaw-
ing out a frozen snake in an act of kindness and then getting
bitten. Within the bounds of safety, however, being kind will
bring you great rewards.

One day, I was sitting in my car at a stoplight when I saw
a strange-looking creature on a bike in my rearview mirror. My
first reaction was to ignore him. He looked like he was in his
fifties, and he was dressed just like a little child playing cowboy.
He rode right up to the stoplight, which seemed to be taking

a very long time to change to green, and he was now parallel with my open window on the passenger side of the car. I turned and smiled at him, and in return he smiled a beatific smile and said, "Greetings from the Master." I was so astonished at what I heard that of course I had to ask, "What?" So he repeated it: "Greetings from the Master." I said thank you and continued smiling. The light changed, and I swear he just disappeared. The feeling I had after this greeting can only be explained as a peak experience. I felt so tremendously happy and joyful I almost had to stop the car. Later I realized that if I hadn't acknowledged this stranger I would have missed a marvelous experience.

Sometimes, being aware of the ways of angels seems like belonging to a secret society where you never know when, where, and how another member of the organization will show up. If you feel like being rude or unkind to a stranger, be careful; he or she just might be an angel. Angels like to appear randomly at various locations to test our reactions. They usually do this in places you wouldn't normally identify with angels, such as gas stations, bars, airports, movie theaters, and street corners. The test itself is not serious. If we miss it or fail it, we have nothing to worry about. The only reason angels do random testing is to teach us love and respect for all human beings. They also want to wake us up to happiness and the joy of being alive.

Angels may give you hints or signs of an impending test. Things to watch for include an intense feeling of lightness in their presence; some form of radiance shining out from behind their eyes and face like one big smile; a knowing look—as if they knew you and you knew them from somewhere; a feeling of timelessness, as if you were suddenly in a movie or a different reality; a very distinctive, mirthful laugh, almost like tinkling bells and extremely contagious; a feeling that all the worldly events around you are ridiculous; and a stirring, sweet aroma resembling jasmine left behind after they disappear.

I bet that many of you have met angels without realizing it. Think back on any experiences you've had that seemed inexplicable, illogical, mysterious, or inconsequential at the time, and see if they fit the angel-testing paradigm. If they do, try to enjoy them *now* and get ready for more. Practice for the future. Many are called but few are chosen for random angel testing. So be prepared!

Chapter 30

The Angel Beauty and Health Program

Every night and every morning thank your own Guardian Angel for peace and for the regeneration of all the cells in your body, and for joy.

Dorie D'Angelo

Mental gravity is the foremost destroyer of health and beauty. Mental gravity equals stress. Stress in the form of negative thoughts, negative circumstances, worries, and tension weighs down your spirit. Beauty and mental gravity are negatively correlated. This means that when the mental gravity load goes up, beauty goes down. Stressed-out people seem to age faster than normal. The process can be reversed if stress and mental gravity are taken away and replaced with spiritual relaxation, lightness, and harmony.

Some people show stress in their faces, some in their bodies, and some in their voices. I call some of the people I know shape shifters. Their shape (body) changes with the outward conditions in their lives. Some days they look like vibrant, youthful spirits, and the next day they look about twenty years older—wrinkled, sunken, and tense.

Angels can help alleviate the problem of mental gravity in our lives. Angels do this by bringing us awareness of our unnecessary worries and, by providing creative solutions to problems that consume time and energy. (All of the methods described in Part Three help lighten mental gravity in one way or another.)

When people remove the seriousness of survival issues from their lives and replace this with living happily in the now, they will naturally become beautiful and radiant. Nuns are known to look much younger than they are and to have very few wrinkles, if any, on their faces. This is because they have given up the ways of the world (such as material possessions and worrying about meals and bills and emotional relationships) for a spiritual life of prayer and service; this shows on their faces. (Of course, this description represents an ideal and not all nuns have the true luxury of a spiritual life.)

It is not feasible for most of us to lead a life of prayer and constant spiritual practice, but there *are* ways to integrate beauty and spirituality into our everyday lives and in turn to radiate more beauty. Meditation is a practice that can keep you young and help you reduce the ill effects of stress. Meditating for as little as twenty minutes a day can reduce the stress that shows up in your face and body. Listening to a relaxation tape can be helpful. When you use these practices, visualize beautiful angels transmitting beauty into your soul. Also, when you look in the mirror, see your face as young and beautiful. Shift the shape in your mind if you want a change; imagine the face of your most beautiful angel superimposed on your own reflection in the mirror.

Physical release like exercise is also a way to reduce mental gravity. You may find this hard to believe, but angels can help you exercise. They can also help you carry things, by lightening the load. One day, I was carrying a heavy table top down some stairs, and I decided to do an experiment. I asked the angels to help me carry it—to make it lighter. It worked! The table top became lighter and easier to carry. Then one day I was hiking up a hill; it became very strenuous at one point, so again I asked the angels to help me. I suddenly felt like an energy force was gently pushing me from behind and releasing my focus on how difficult the climb was. You can try this with every form of physical movement. If you are a dancer, imagine that the angels are lifting you up and making you one with the music. (Maybe this was Fred Astaire's secret!)

Angels can also help you if you are on a diet. You might think this is going a bit too far—angels helping you cut back on food? I know someone who lost weight and kept if off and who gives the angels credit for this feat. I admit that one subject does not make a scientific study, but I know others who are trying this now and experiencing success. I think this works for two reasons. First, when you ask the angels to help you accomplish something, they know you are ready for success and will stick to the program. They assist you by distracting you from eating too much and by helping you change your eating habits. Second, angels help you go after what the food has been replacing in your life. If it is love and romance, they will lead you on the right path to fulfillment, which means they help make you aware of the blocks and problems that are keeping you from what you really want.

Angels don't eat food, but they can put on the appearance of a feast for you. Imagine angels having a great party, drinking nectar and eating angel food cake with delight and merriment. They're having a wonderful time gobbling up enormous chunks of angel food, which is really just foam, or thin air, or imagination. This will make you feel so silly that you won't want to eat for some time.

Angels will lighten the field of gravity around you. This will help you in all the areas of your life. It will enable you to display your true natural beauty, and it will keep you healthier.

Chapter 31

Cosmic Jokers: Archetypes of Evil

Legend has it that the father of evil was once God's second in command, chief among all his angels, the beautiful and beloved archangel Lucifer. Lucifer means "light bearer," and Lucifer was to be a teacher to humanity. God needed a volunteer to come to earth to strengthen and enlighten mankind through the use of tests and temptations. Lucifer volunteered. He began to delight in the tests he was giving. Eventually, he was testing humanity not for God but to feed his own pride. And, in feeding his own pride, he created a separation between himself and God. So God kicked him out of heaven. He had to go somewhere, so he created hell.

Eventually, Lucifer became identified as the deceiver (an independent force to destroy humanity). Legend also has it that Lucifer took other angels out of heaven along with him—hence the fallen angels (or cosmic jokers). Lucifer is also known to some as Satan. *The Dictionary of Angels,* by Gustav Davidson, lists Satan as a fallen angel having nothing to do with the archangel

Lucifer. Other books make no distinction between the two. *Satan* is the Hebrew word for *adversary*, and Satan is an adversary to God's love. For Satan, love is something foreign to fight against.

The debate of good and evil strikes a different note in all of us. I have read many books that dismiss evil as something we make up in our minds that manifests in our lives only because we let it and that has no real life force of its own. I used to think that there weren't any real victims on this planet. Now I think that we need to expand our language and come up with several different words to represent the various types of victims that *do* exist. The reason that victims are victims is because of a force that is evil. Regardless of whether we ourselves create this force, it is as real as its victims.

It is difficult to ignore the concept of good versus evil. It is the theme of many movies and books, and it is the theme of many human lives. This battle of the dark versus the light goes on around us all the time. But when it goes on inside us and divides our own being, we are weakened, off balance, and unintegrated.

The fear that if we are not "good" we will be punished can start to haunt people who are doing their best to be good. But who is going to carry out this punishment? God does not punish. God gave us free will and cannot punish us even if we won't accept God's help. And God cannot stop us from punishing ourselves and others. Free will means that God won't interfere, not even when the force of evil is after us. The only thing God will do is offer us unconditional love, and this love can be our refuge at any time we need it. The catch is that *we* have to *ask* for God's love and be open to it.

The Cosmic Joker Syndrome

Cosmic jokers are the fallen angels, or you could call them demons if you like. Cosmic jokers help us punish ourselves when we think we have done something bad or wrong. They don't do this by addressing the obvious; they get to us through our humanness and our pride. Cosmic jokers are not very angelic; they exist to test and punish. They work out the consequences of our negative beliefs and toy with our egomaniacal fantasies. The trick is to spot the humor in their little games and get away from them. They only understand practical jokes, ones that are not on them but on us. Furthermore, they have no understanding of love. So if we fall prey to a cosmic joke, the best thing we can do is increase self-love and acceptance.

Cosmic jokers are brats who teach us to laugh at ourselves through their practical jokes. We may have to eat some large slices of humble pie before we realize how funny we are. If we are too serious, fearful, obsessive, hateful, or prejudiced, the cosmic jokers have a field day teaching us lessons. If we dabble too long in darkness, or in an altered state of mind resulting from ingesting chemical substances or deprivation of sleep, the cosmic jokers will get us with their bratty lessons. We give them the power by weakening ourselves with fear and loathing. Their lessons can have a positive outcome by guiding us back on track, the track of awareness and awakeness. But it is up to us to find the positive side of these lessons. Cosmic jokers can be ruthless, just like Lucifer's original group of fallen angels.

Keep in mind that we all have our little battles, and when we get sidetracked by them we open ourselves up to negative consequences; it helps to be aware of these traps, so that our awareness can give us a choice. We attract the cosmic jokers when we fall into some of the following traps.

If we have a "worst fear" trap, one that haunts us and makes us superstitious, the jokers may choose to cultivate this fear for us. Fears come in many shapes, sizes, magnitudes, and conditions. Fear is a powerful negative force, one that can consume your spiritual energy. When we spend our energy on fear, we make it worse. Fear varies profoundly in each of us, and it is difficult to understand how deeply our fears can dig into our souls. If you have a fear haunting you, start to examine and confront it. Tell it in no uncertain terms to get the hell out! If we attach power to our fears by being superstitious, then the cosmic jokers have no choice except to use that power to make a joke. Get to the point where you can laugh at your fears, and then they won't have the power to destroy otherwise peaceful moments.

If we fall into the trap of taking ourselves too seriously, we will be the brunt of several cosmic jokes. Being serious means that we have great concern over everything. Comedy makes fun of serious behavior; that is what makes good comedy. Think about Jackie Gleason's character Ralph on the "Honeymooners." The humor in the show came from situations Ralph took too seriously, and at the end of each episode Alice helped Ralph laugh at himself with love. Seriousness is also the trap of thinking we are always right, and many times the joke is on us.

Cosmic jokers also love to play with the trap of prejudices and expecations in any form. The prejudice or expectation may be about race, religion, occupation, or gender, or it may even be one you don't realize you have. Whatever we prejudge will be fair game for the cosmic jokers. If you are prejudiced against a certain race of people, the jokers may see to it that you or your child marries someone of that race. Or you may have a dramatic experience of someone from a religion you don't respect rescuing you or your child from danger. The lesson is simple: Don't judge! Each situation with each human being exists as it exists, so expect the unexpected or cease expectations and gain everything.

If you are obsessed over something or someone, you are just asking for trouble. Obsession is the seduction of your mind by some desired or feared object. The value you have placed on this desired or feared object is skewed in an unrealistic fashion. You may have obsessive thoughts that haunt you throughout the day. The bottom line is that obsession disturbs your peace. And the cosmic jokers will only make it worse by giving you confusing signs and indications about the object of your obsession. Obsessions can get so bad that we may need professional help, and when it has gotten that bad it is difficult for us to realize help is needed. Common, everyday obsessions are something we can get rid of ourselves; this process depends on a sense of humor toward the obsessive behavior. When obsessions become a trap in your life, return to simplicity. Release the obsession: Who cares whether you locked your door or not—just send some angels over to house-sit if you are worried. If you are in a state of obsession over another human being, release him or her; if he or she comes back to you than take your cue.

Cosmic jokers are quite creative in playing with humans "under the influence." We may be under the influence of chemical substances (for example, LSD, alcohol, tranquilizers, and pain killers) or we may be under the influence of sensory deprivation or of not having had enough sleep or the right foods. When we move ourselves into an altered state of consciousness, we sometimes step into cosmic joker territory. The cosmic jokers turn into a movie crew, to make a movie—not necessarily for your enjoyment—with you in the leading role. You might find yourself in a science-fiction movie complete with aliens, or in a horror film complete with demons and monsters. Or you might be cast as the king of time and space or as a spiritual mystic who has cosmic consciousness and becomes one with all creation. These movies seem real, but look at who the directors and producers are. They are the cosmic jokers, and they will oblige you in acting out your fantasies and fears until they seem real. Sooner or later, however, you may get sick of being an actor in these epic thrillers and want to get back to a consensus reality. You've realized you have had enough of the lessons the extraterrestrials and dark characters have to teach. Welcome back; it was all a joke: You are simply you, not the king of time and space, not the victim of aliens and monsters—just good old you. All is well; now you are back in your own movie as director (with your higher self as producer), and you have stories of different worlds to tell and pictures to paint.

I have talked to people who have had cosmic jokers appear to them. This is unusual, but it can happen. It only happens from a source of deep fear. Seeing the image of a demon or ghost can be quite frightening and elicits more fear. Fear gives these beings power, so the best thing to do if you see one is to get centered, take a deep breath, and then tell them and the fear to leave. Release the fear by taking refuge in something sacred to you. For example, Christians can use the name of Jesus or the image of a cross. The affirmation to the archangel Michael (found in Part Five) recited three times is also very effective.

The only reason I am adding this chapter on cosmic jokers to the book is that more people have experienced their antics than I originally thought. I think it is important to address the power of what negative thought patterns can do in a worst-case scenario. Whether people really see or hear cosmic jokers or whether this is just their imagination does not matter. What does matter is the stress and fear in their lives that brought them to that point. Unconditional love is the one and only true cure for every negative thing imaginable. If you can't find this love from another human or yourself, find it from God and the angels. The angels will never let you down if you open your heart to them. They will teach you to love yourself unconditionally, and this in turn will draw in love from the world around you.

Chapter 32

Reminders About Life on Earth

Truth is a pathless land. (There is no need to seek it through any occult hierarchy, any guru, any doctrine. . . .) The important thing is to free your mind of envy, hate, and violence; and for that you don't need an organization.
                                                                J. Krishnamurti

The main themes I've been stressing in this book are that life is not to be taken seriously, that we need to play more, and that we can learn to be happy-go-lucky with a little training. This is much easier said than done. Changing our thought patterns requires training and effort on our parts. To get anywhere near a state of enlightened grace, we must be willing to grow and to do our spiritual work. Angels are guides and teachers, but they will not do or interfere in work we must do for ourselves. Sometimes our work is not very fun and can create discomfort, but this only means we are changing and awakening to our highest personality and happiness.

Change can create a certain amount of pain and upset in our lives. The pain and upset that results from change is growing pain. When growth brings pain, we can either "*go* through the pain, or *grow* through the pain." Changing our way of thinking so that we can be happier and more awake in life may entail going back in the past and healing or letting go of pain we stored as a child or young adult; instead of just going through it again, we can grow through it. To become less critical of ourselves, we must remove pride and take a good look at our lives through loving eyes.

The ideas in this book about how angels help us create heaven in our lives are for people who are not afraid to experience growing pain and who are not afraid to give their burdens over to a higher power. People can laugh even while they're in pain; it isn't easy, but if you practice on a regular basis you can master the technique. Pain is a teacher. Pain teaches us to let go and not be so attached to emotional burdens. Avoiding pain is a human instinct; we tend to put pain aside for later and ignore it at precisely the time when it is easiest to confront. Don't worry about it! There is always a way out, and seeking loving divine humor is the best shortcut I know.

If you visualize yourself on a path to enlightenment in this lifetime, go easy on yourself and take along the angels. Burst out laughing at every new growth point on your path. In this New Age, we have many choices and opportunities presented to us in the name of spiritual growth. Explore where the information is coming from and whether it really fits into your path. If you choose to have psychic readings (aura readings, tarot card readings, past-life readings, or astrological counseling), beware of the limitations of this sort of information. Too often, information from a psychic reading turns into a self-fulfilling prophecy, because we are all suggestible to some degree. If the information doesn't seem right to you or is something that you don't want in your life, rise above it.

Rise above it by knowing that you have free will and can create miracles in your life. Go for the highest potential in your life.

If a psychic tells you something you don't like, use this information as a gauge for the middle point. That is, say to yourself, "If I only want to go halfway with my life, this is probably what I'll end up doing, but if I go all the way to the top there are no limits to what I can achieve." Sometimes, psychic information relates to doubts and fears we have in the present. When the information is confirmed by a psychic reading of our present state of affairs, our doubts and fears are reinforced.

Keep in mind that, in time, you always get what you really want. Realize how ridiculous it is to believe, on the one hand, that anything is possible and that miracles of love can happen, and then to turn around and limit those thoughts by listening to the advice given in a psychic reading of your future.

With the angels' help, you can visualize and create the future as you want it. Angels won't give you past-life information or tell you about your future. They will give you this-life inspiration to live your life fully and happily in the present tense. When you get your information from the realm of heaven, the highest of spiritual planes, only you, God, and the angels are involved. The information you receive will never take away or interfere with your free will. The information will set you free, free from the projections and expectations other humans have on you. Information from heaven will inspire you to become strong, creative, and centered within yourself, so that your choices and decisions will benefit you and those around you.

Finally, the insight and advice in this book is directed toward people who are basically mentally healthy and who function well in their world. If you are going through pain that is not easily removed or you are blocked by compulsive behavior, it never hurts to talk to a trained professional, such as a good analyst or counselor. Be sure to ask the angels to lead you to the right type of outside help. Look for someone loving and experienced. The reason I recommend finding someone other than yourself to help you is because one requirement for keeping ourselves healthy (besides getting the right vitamins) is loving contact and relationship with other members of our species.

Part Five

Angel Forum
and Annex

Chapter 33

Angel Personality Profiles

The Angel that presided o'er my birth,
said "Little creature formed of Joy & Mirth,
go and love without the help of anything on earth."

William Blake

Human Angels and Aspiring Angels

Angels are formed of God's joy and mirth. Sometimes they love humans so much, they decide to become one. They might do this with a specific intention, such as helping the humans they love achieve happiness. Or they may want to assist in a global mission. The choice to become human is a risk, because then they have to abide in the human body and experience the emotional turmoil humans go through at times. Because they are highly evolved and extremely sensitive, angels may have adverse reactions to the everyday life of humans. Psychic repair and help comes from realizing their connection to the heavenly circuit. They must go and love spiritually without the help of anything on earth. They made the choice to be humans, and now they must stay linked to God's unconditional love so that they don't self-destruct.

Human angels are optimistic about human ideals. They chose to be a human to experience the joys of being human, so they will do their best to live a full life. The funny thing is that they haven't yet got it down, so to speak, and they sometimes get themselves into humorous situations. They always seem to be in the process of learning the language of human behavior. Children experience them as kindred spirits in this learning process. Children and babies are drawn to human angels.

Human angels are naturally charming, sweet, gracious, loving, and witty, and they love a good laugh. Life for them is about the joy of the moment. They feel an affinity for angelic ideals and want to arrange a happy ending for everyone. Human angels expect and seek to see the forms of heaven all around them, wherever they go on planet earth.

Human angels know that they are protected and guarded on earth. The number thirteen is always lucky for them. They have a practice of turning all superstitious beliefs to work in their favor. Their lives are full of synchronistic events and favorable coincidences. In essence, they lead charmed lives, because they know how to attract love and happiness to themselves.

Their homes may be decorated in the heavenly colors of an abalone shell. They display rocks, pebbles, stones, gems, shells, or fossils somewhere in their house. This habit deepens their connection to the earth realm, the realm in which devas, elves, and fairies play, and helps keep them grounded. Otherwise, they would have a tendency to want to float away into the ethers.

Light is a constant in the life of a human angel. If the lighting isn't right in a room, they will not be comfortable until they can design and sculpture it the right way. Human angels reflect light off their bodies in a powerful or unusual way, noticeable in sunlight, moonlight, and candlelight, and in photographs. They often talk about light — the light of the sun, neon lights, lighting, prisms, crystals, pink light, items that glow in the dark, and moonlight on water or snow.

You will often find human angels looking up at the sky and noticing magnificent birds in places you don't expect, clouds that look like angels, rainbows when there hasn't been rain, an abundance of shooting stars at night, and strange beautiful sights you can't explain. Human angels have a reverence for beautiful things, like moonbeams, sunsets, and nature at its finest.

If you feel like a human angel or a human aspiring to be an angel, keep in mind that your help comes from heaven. This means that if you get exasperated with being human, you must remember you chose this to help enlighten up the humans here on earth. You loved them so much you decided to become one. Or, you have decided to create your humanness into angelhood. Either way, remember that your goal is to bring heaven and lightness to earth, and remember that you are now human and must abide by the lessons your humanness will provide.

CLUES TO HUMAN ANGELS AND ASPIRING ANGELS

1. You feel light and airy at times, and you are convinced you could fly or float up through the clouds.
2. You have experiences of heavenly joy and lightness that leave you laughing hysterically.
3. You see other humans and yourself as innocent, and it is easy for you to forgive and forget.
4. You have trouble taking the concept of money seriously; you are inclined to play all the time rather than to be motivated by money.
5. At times you find yourself lovingly observing life as if you were invisible. Occasionally, adults seem to see right past you as if you were transparent. Children and babies always notice you and are drawn to you in a special way.

If you resonated with one or more of these clues, then you have definite angel tendencies. You can develop them further with the help of this book and the help of your spiritual brothers and sisters in heaven, the angels.

Sensitives

Everyone is sensitive to some degree, but a *sensitive* is someone who is ultrasensitive. Being a sensitive is not very easy at times. Sensitives receive impressions easily and quickly. They receive impressions that others miss. They start to feel responsible for having received a strong inner knowledge about something or someone. Their intuition is extremely keen, to the point where they purposely doubt it at times, so as not to be burdened. Sensitives are usually highly intelligent and creative, but, being so sensitive, it can be difficult for them to bring forth their gifts and face possible rejection and other adverse conditions.

Some sensitives can take on another human being's physical pain and sensations, or feel another's emotional hurt sometimes more deeply than the person truly experiencing it. This may force the sensitives to go on autopilot, creating an automatic routine to protect themselves from feeling too much. This isn't necessary. Sensitives can learn to understand themselves, and they can learn ways of removing themselves from another's pain without going on autopilot.

Sensitives are attracted to the ideals and thought patterns of the New Age movement, or to other forms of religious and philosophical idealism and mysticism. Sensitives who want to understand themselves are inclined to seek past-life information and psychic readings about their future. This need for a feeling of certainty and guidance can become a problem in itself. Card readings and other information given through psychics can become a crutch or an addiction; worse yet, such practices can keep you from living fully in the present as captain of your own ship. Eventually, sensitives may find that the New Age is just not enough for some reason; something is missing.

One reason for this sense that something is missing may be

that they have lost sight of their initial reasons for exploring the New Age. If they were looking for spiritual truth in different directions because organized religion left them cold, they may find that they are still left cold. Sensitives want the truth, but at times they get sidetracked because they are so sensitive, sus- ceptible, and psychic. Sensitives need to love and accept their sensitivity as a special gift and learn to fine-tune their gift so that it serves them and those around them.

The sensitives' higher self resembles that of a saint. They came to learn similar lessons, and their inner nature is similar. Their houses may even have the feeling of a mission, monastery, or chapel. The problems of the sick, the homeless, and the impov- erished can either drive them to work in one of the helping pro- fessions or overwhelm them to the point that they don't even want to go out their front door. On the high side, sensitives may be able to lapse into states where they have beatific visions and mystic raptures that leave them with feelings of awe, reverence, and perfection.

Sensitives are very gifted in the fine arts. The problem is that their sensitivity and saintly natures keep them from sharing their gifts—often for fear of rejection or fear of success for which they feel unworthy. Sensitives can use angels to help them understand themselves better and to develop tools for their own growth and for living successfully in the often insensitive world around them. Angels can help sensitives develop their gifts so they can share them and enrich the world around them. Also, sensitives some- times need armor, and the angels can provide the armor for protecting them in everyday life on earth. Angels can help sen- sitives become the ultrahumans they are meant to be.

CLUES TO THE SENSITIVE PERSONALITY

1. You find yourself merging with others to the point where you can feel their physical and emotional pain. You feel sorry for everyone, not just for yourself.
2. You seem to be psychic, and you pick up impressions easily.

Very often you think something and the person you're with will say it, or vice versa.

3. People frequently remark on your extreme sensitivity.
4. Experiencing life can be completely overwhelming at times, to the point where you have to space out or "give up."
5. You are attracted to astrology, psychic readings, tarot cards, metaphysical phenomena, and you like dark bedrooms for isolation and restoration.
6. You have a strong, ineffable sense of the truth. You know, but you do not say.

If you resonated with any of the statements above, then you are a sensitive. This book was written to help you the sensitive enjoy life more and develop your gifts and creativity to their highest good. Part Five lists some other books that might be of interest to you. Please use the angels for your psychic repair and learn to trust yourself. All the answers lie within you; all you have to do is trust. You have everything it takes to be an ultrahuman, so bring in the angels and you will be on your way.

Chapter 34

Practicing Love and Kindness

To love for the sake of being loved is human,
but to love for the sake of loving is Angelic.
                                    Alphonse de Lamartine

I asked my four-year-old niece to tell me what she knew about angels. She told me, "They probably glow in the dark. . . . And, of course, we know they have feet." But most important she told me she knew that angels love little kids. I agreed, and I asked her, since she was a little kid, if the angels had any messages for all of us here on earth. She quickly replied, "Yes. Be kind for another, and love one another!"

Soon after she gave me this message, I had the chance to hear the Dalai Lama speak. The Dalai Lama is the spiritual leader of the Tibetan Buddhists, and he is living in exile from his homeland. The overall feeling emanating from the entire audience lifted my soul from the minute I walked into the building—I felt like I was floating in an ocean of love. I had the privilege of sitting near the front of the auditorium, where the Tibetan families were sitting. The look on their faces when the Dalai Lama came out to speak was incredibly moving, and I felt like I had merged into their world. I felt a sense of true compassion even before I knew this would be the subject of the Dalai Lama's talk.

Basically, the Dalai Lama had the same message for us humans that my niece relayed from the angels. The title of his talk was "A Human Approach to World Peace." He talked about practicing compassion for others as a way to develop inner stability and a sense of responsibility for the human family. Compassion provides security and inner stamina and allows us to reduce fear and develop self-confidence with awareness. What the Dalai Lama means by compassion is actually altruism. When you show kindness and act upon a feeling of empathy toward a very poor person, your compassion is based on altruistic considerations. On the other hand, love toward your partner, lover, spouse, friend, or children is usually based on attachment. When the attachment changes, your kindness also changes (and may even disappear). Real love is not based on attachment, but on altruism.

The Dalai Lama said that the main source of supreme happiness and joy is mental stability and mental peace. Several things can interfere with mental peace. One such thing is anger. The Dalai Lama said that anger diminishes mind—that it is of no use at all and appears as protection from something that *might* happen. Anger deceives us. A person can destroy your property, your body, your friends, and all the supposed sources of your happiness, but real mental stability and peace of mind cannot be destroyed, unless your brain is physically injured. We are minds; we are consciousness. The real enemy to our peace of mind is not external but internal, such as anger.

The foundation for solving human problems lies in transforming human attitudes. If we are happy, truly happy without external reasons, with our minds at peace, then we can give kindness and love to other people effortlessly because we are drawing upon an unlimited source.

I felt compelled to share this information with you because it sums up the angels' message for us. First and foremost, the angels want us to know that we must find our own center within ourselves—the place where we no longer need to judge everything as good or bad and where anger does not interfere with our inner peace. With mental stability comes true peace and happiness. With true peace and happiness comes the drive to be kind to ourselves and love ourselves, so in turn we can love and be kind to others. This is truly the first step toward world peace. This is a crucial and timely message. We must not continue selfishly destroying and overpopulating the earth for a short lifetime of supposed happiness, only to leave the earth in a worse state for our grandchildren and our grandchildren's children.

I don't want to detract from the simplicity of the original message, so I will leave it to you to arrive at your own mental peace and stability. I hope this book will prove helpful in some way. The message is timeless and transcends all cultural and physical barriers. So, please, let it start with you: "Be kind for another, and love one another"—now, before it is too late. Let this be your call to become an angelic force on earth.

I would like to thank Frankie Lee Slater for loaning me her notes from the Dalai Lama's lecture.

Chapter 35

The Angel Forum

The angel forum in this chapter presents an open discussion on angels. In it, a variety of people express their points of view on angels. Their stories illustrate the various ways angels interact with human beings. The topics and opinions expressed do not necessarily match my own. And the people expressing their views do not necessarily agree with everything I've written in this book. The first contribution is a poem written by my eight-year-old niece.

Angel Poem
  by Elizabeth Ann Godfrey

Angels are very holy and they are ten feet tall.
They wear beautiful white dresses and a halo.
They guide you every minute of the day.
Even though you can't see them, they are still here.
And I know you can't put your hand out and touch them.
They make you happy when you are sad.
Angels help and love you very much.

*Sometimes in pictures Angels have wings, but I'm not sure if
    they have wings in real life.
They live on the earth with you, except they're still in heaven, too.
I know it's confusing to you—it's confusing to me, too!*

Attracting Love and Romance
by Mary Beth Crain

Whenever I think of calling in the angels to do my romantic
bidding, I remember an episode of "Gilligan's Island" in which
the professor builds a large robot that supposedly does everything you ask. Of course, everybody on the island agrees that
the robot should build a boat that can take them all home. They
all pack up, say their farewells, and meet on shore at dawn.
Sure enough, the robot has followed instructions and designed
a luxury liner. The only problem is that it's about twelve inches
long. "Whoops," says the professor. "I guess I forgot to give him
the dimensions."

Never forget to give the angels the dimensions. Because, as
we all know by now, our metaphysical friends are incorrigible
funsters and only need the smallest excuse to turn the drama
of our lives into one big cosmic joke. They try to put a lid on
it, and sometimes God or Mother Mary or a particular saint
known for something sobering, like gruesome martyrdom, is
called in to give them a talking to when their little pranks get
out of hand.

At least I hope that's what happened when I prayed for a man
who really loved me to come along, and I got somebody who
wore cologne that smelled like bug spray and who had a big,
fat wife nobody, not even the angels, would want to tangle with,
in alleys either dark or light.

Needless to say, this was distressing. Not only was I completely repulsed by the answer to my prayers, but his obsession
knew no bounds. There were gifts, cards, phone calls, entreaties.

I wanted to run off to Gilligan's Island myself, just to escape him.

At my wit's end, I called Terry Taylor, who told me that it was definitely time for an angel conference. I told her that I thought it was definitely time for angel reform school. But I called in my angel of love and romance, and our conversation went something like this.

Me: Thanks a bunch!

ALR: Well, you asked for a man who really loved you.

Me: But he wears bug spray!

ALR: Sorry. You didn't specify.

Me: Specify? Just how specific do we have to get here?

ALR: As specific as you need to be to attract the right person.

Me: Listen, you guys are supposed to know everything I'm thinking anyway.

ALR: We want *you* to know what you're thinking. To be very clear about it. Otherwise the things you attract will be slightly off base.

Me: I guess I'm lucky you didn't send me a chimpanzee or something.

ALR: Go back and meditate on the man you really want. See him, feel him, call on him. We'll get the message.

Me: Just make sure *he* gets the message. Okay?

ALR: Scout's honor.

Me: Your fingers are crossed.

ALR: Whoops. Didn't think you'd notice.

Believe me, you have to watch these guys. Anyway, I went back and thought about where I'd gone wrong. I'd asked for an older man who shared all my interests, who was spiritually inclined and passionate, and who had a career of his own. But I hadn't specified marital status, and I hadn't specified that I should be equally attracted to him. You'd think the angels would assume such obvious details, but no. You absolutely have to spell it out.

So, I did another meditation. I got relaxed, felt golden white light coming through me from my toes to my nose, went to my favorite mental imaging place, which happens to be a grassy field by a beautiful stream, and imagined my perfect mate. I saw his face and his eyes; I felt his gentle, unconditional love. I made a list of all his qualities, and I made sure that he smelled nice and didn't have a wife the size of Mount Rushmore. Then I mentally summoned my angel of love and romance.

"That's him," I said. "Bring him to me. And no fooling around!"

Well, it took about six months. But I can cheerfully report that at the present time I am the proud companion of an adorable and adoring seventy-year-old man, who shares my interests, has a career of his own, is deeply religious, unmarried, and wears a cologne that knocks my socks off. In fact, I met him on Christmas day, at mass, which only goes to show you that when the angels decide to do things right they put on the whole show.

Of course, there's a bit more to attracting love and romance than just programming your angels. You have to feel good about yourself. You have to feel that you deserve the best. And you have to pay attention. One of my favorite cartoons shows a woman sitting on a rock, contemplating her Prince Charming. "Some day my prince will come," she daydreams away. "He'll be handsome and perfect, and he'll sweep me off my feet. . . ." And presently a man rides up on a white horse. "Excuse me," he says. But the woman doesn't hear him. She's too busy fantasizing about her prince. "Excuse me," the man says again. "I'm Prince Charming." But the woman is totally oblivious to him. "And he'll have blond hair, and he'll love to dance, and . . ." she's still going on. And with a sigh, Prince Charming turns his horse around and trots off.

So you have to notice when the angels send you someone. And then you have to work at the relationship, because nothing comes free, especially when the angels are involved in it. They like to see you earn your keep. In my case, the man I loved was very shy, and I had to work like the dickens to make him comfortable with me. In fact, there were more than a few moments when I was ready to declare defeat. But in every meditation I did, the angels confirmed that yes, this was the one. I just wasn't to lose faith. And sure enough, one day a miracle happened and he asked me, very shyly, if I might like to play golf with him, and life has been one big birdie ever since.

Oh, yes, here's another thing you might try if you're having relationship questions and you want "yes" or "no" confirmation from the angels. Just ask them to send you a sign that the person is or isn't the one the universe has picked out for you. In my case, I asked for the angels to send me a rose to confirm that this fellow was "the one." And about five days later, a nun friend of mine and I met for lunch and the first thing she did was to hand me a novena card of St. Therese. I opened it up and there, inside, was the sweetest little pink rose.

Big chill time! "Jan," I said, "Why are you giving me this?"

"It was the funniest thing," she replied. "But yesterday I was driving and I got lost and I ended up at a hospital run by an order of sisters devoted to St. Therese. There was a chapel in the hospital, with a shrine to St. Therese and roses all around it. And suddenly I felt I had to pray for you, that God gives you a relationship that's beautiful, fulfilling, and challenging. And I picked this rose from the shrine."

So the angels are listening. Just keep an eye on them because, as I've said, their humor can sometimes be more than you bargained for. Actually, I think they may have written the entire "Gilligan's Island" series, and that they rerun it down in hell, for eternity. So I'm going to be very good from this day forth. Aren't you?

On Angels
by Francis Jeffrey

(1) JEFFREY'S SCIENTIFIC THOUGHTS ABOUT ANGELS

Angels and ideas

Angels are creatures of imagination. This does not mean that they are any less real than you are. Some esoteric teachers have said to their students, "You are nothing but an idea!" To which certain students have repleid, "Yes, but I'm a real good idea."

As Shakespeare said, "We are such stuff as dreams are made of." And angels are evidently made of the same stuff as the non-material aspect of ourselves. Angels can thus coexist with us in our individual worlds of ideas, thoughts, and images — where we exist, somehow mysteriously connected with our bodies and usually focused inside our bodies or, more precisely, "in our heads."

Angels in the brain

When philosophers and scientists have thought seriously about the connection between mind and body, they generally have pointed to the brain, and concluded that the brain is where the mind operates (or enters) the body. The brain is composed of a trillion little cells (called neurons), all packed together and tickling each other (chemically) with their tiny tendrils. As a flurry of activity (or conversation) runs through this group, it can produce results that resemble a computer running its program. A program is just a sequence of events, planned in advance, or a sequence of decisions, anticipated in advance. (In this respect, a computer program is not very different from a television program, except that in a television program all the decisions are made in advance, not just anticipated.)

Such "programs" result in what you do, or what you experience.

Now, imagine tiny angels stationed at each of these cells, steering the conversation this way or that. This idea is similar to the model of a guardian angel for a person, only these little angels are guiding individual cells. By giving a little nudge one way or the other, they might introduce a subtle change in your perceptions, or a small, but decisive, change in your behavior.

These tiny angels might do a little ornamental gardening with the tiny tendrils, and thus effect permanent changes in your brain programs. They are then acting as the brain program editors described elsewhere in this book. They will only do this when they are invited in by the person in question. When active, you will probably notice their presence as a warm, fuzzy feeling in the head, as a pink glow around everything you look at, as a melodious echoing of sounds, or as the fragrance of a warm summer's eve when the air is pregnant with the promise of unknown possibilities.

Angels and endorphins

Endorphins are a kind of natural chemical found in the brain; they are associated with pleasure and relief of pain. Actually, it seems that the presence of endorphins increases the brain's ability to "screen its messages"—to tune out unpleasant signals from pain nerves, and to focus your attention wherever you want it to go. Evidently, this freedom to attend as we please to whatever pleases us is the state we call "pleasure." Pain, on the other hand, is some hurt or sick situation *demanding* our attention, and jangling our brain in the process.

Angels can serve the same purpose as endorphins, positioning themselves at key crossroads in the brain, forbidding unwanted signals from passing. Of course, if you decide to use angels in this way, be careful not to get into the syndrome of "angel abuse," where you screen out so much all the time that you get "out of touch."

2) JEFFREY'S UNSCIENTIFIC OBSERVATIONS OF ANGELS

Healing angels

Imagine a globe of radiant light, way off in the heavens. Draw off a pinch of this golden glow, and form it into a tiny angel. Say,

"Hello, angel," and give it a name. Repeat this procedure until you have a whole line of tiny angels streaming toward you through space. Direct them into the part of your body that is unwell or painful. (Or direct them into someone else you wish to heal.) See the angels arrive on the scene and envelope the diseased or injured area, permeating the tissues and cells with their intense, warm golden light—driving out the pain and inflammation.

If the situation is really serious, take the emanantions of golden light from these angels and form it into vaster numbers of smaller angels, who can go to work at the cellular level, treating each cell individually.

If you're fond of the medical model of healing, try an angel I.V. (intravenous injection). Imagine a translucent tube coming down from the angel source, down through space, and into one of your veins (or right into the part of the body that is ill). Tiny angels—drip, drip, drip—float down through this tube and into your body, where they perform their healing activities, as above.

We are certainly not recommending that you substitute this practice for physical treatment in the case of serious, medically diagnosed conditions! Use it to supplement traditional medical care.

SANTA

Flying over Greenland in 1987 on the day of the harmonic convergence, I had a startling revelatory experience. As I gazed out the window of a 747 at 30,000 feet, I spied hoof marks and the tracks of sleigh runners upon the vastly white snow fields. Interesting, I reflected, they're still using sleigh and reindeer down there in Greenland.

Then, as the shadow of our plane fleeted across the path of the tracks, the full impact hit me: Those tracks were enormous! To appear that big viewed from that altitude, the sleigh must have been the size of an aircraft carrier! And the deer must also have been of titanic stature. And who was driving that sleigh?

And then I received the full revelation: Santa Claus! Yes,

of course, that's how he does it! He's huge! Santa has plenty of toys for everyone.

Later I reflected on the true meaning of SANTA, and I realized that it stands for Super Angelic Nocturnal Transport Angel. SANTA is a gigantic angelic being who moves stuff around at night. SANTA is a special-purpose angel assigned to planet earth.

The luminous cloud

Several months after my SANTA revelation, I was in Malibu, California, and a friend at the beach asked me to take my car to pick someone up who wanted to visit but didn't have transportation. This woman—I'll call her "K"—was staying at a house in the mountains.

I drove through the dark winter's night, and, as I looked in the general direction I was heading, I saw something I'd never seen before—something that mystified me. It was a luminous cloud towering above the hills, like a pillar of scintillating, multi-hued pastel light At first, I thought of the aurora borealis, but that is never visible from the temperate latitudes of Los Angeles and, besides, this tower of light was clearly a local phenomenon.

The road wound through the mountains, and I could see it was bringing me closer and closer to the luminous cloud. I wondered if I would finally arrive at its base—like the end of the rainbow?

At last, the road turned beside a steep hillside, which blocked my immediate view of the tower of light. There, on the hillside, I found the appointed address. The house was totally dark.

I beeped the car horn, and soon there emerged a tall figure in a white robe, carrying a flashlight, and beckoning me up the path. The robe the woman was wearing turned out to be a bathrobe. She thanked me for coming and apologized that she was not quite ready to go, because the lights had gone out some time ago and she was unable to locate the fuse box.

I helped her find the fuse box and restore the electricity. When the lights came back on, I saw a tall blond woman who bore a certain resemblance to Brigette Nielsen.

On our way down to the beach in my car, "K" started telling me about angels. She spoke of them most matter-of-factly. She had been in close contact with them for years. In her meditations, she drew them around her, and as a cloud they clung to here wherever she would go. In my little car, I could feel this was true. (Later, over a dinner with our mutual friend, "K" seemed more like a normal, sophisticated woman. I learned that she was on vacation from her home in the snowy wilds of Canada.)

Several days later, drawn by a notable chain of coincidences to travel hundreds of miles, I was to meet a very angelic-looking young woman named "T," who had vague plans to write a book about angels!

Healing With Angels
by Linda Zwingeberg Fickes

All healers, be they microsurgeons, dentists, acupuncturists, or evangelical faith healers, work with the healing angels of the body. They must work with nature. Nature is life with intelligence.

An angel is simply an intelligence of Nature that guides a spark of life toward its perfect fulfillment. An angel may oversee the life spark of a cell in the body, an organ, the physical, mental, or emotional body, or the soul, the Inner Christ, or the I Am body.

An angel may be tiny or vast. But each angel has the quality of perfect synchronism with the good of that life and the good of all. No healing proceeds without the angels' care. Man, the "healer," simply removes the obstacles and opens the doors, so the angels can do their work.

The angel or intelligence that oversees the physical body directs and coordinates the angels that make up that body — the angels of the skin, blood, nervous system, and so forth. This angelic being also interacts with the angels of all our subtle bodies. The subtler the body, the closer to God and the more powerful and simpler the angelic life within that body.

All the subtle bodies are guided by their own natural tendency or intelligence. The mental body is composed of thoughts and ideas, each one of which has an angel to fulfill it.

The emotional body is a subtle body composed of emotional energy flows. Each flow of emotion has a guiding angel. When these angels are restricted, life gets bottled up. The energy becomes frustrated and consequently affects the grosser mental and physical bodies. Many therapists are discovering how to allow the emotional angels to assist in the process of emotional energy release, which always concludes with love.

The etheric body or soul is the perfect and original blueprint for an individual's existence. Therefore, it carries the original design matrix created for it by God. Look for the angels of the etheric or soul's body, and you will see a fine geometric matrix of stars. The stars set a tone of perfection and harmony for every part of our being.

On the Inner Christ level, beyond the soul, the body is still less complex and made up of the qualities of universal love and compassion. When we connect consciously with our own universal intentions, the Christ angels will help us fulfill them.

The I Am subtle body is even closer to God and therefore simpler and more powerful. On the I Am level, we find the pure qualities of our own God being. A feeding of energy from this level might be: "I Am Power," "I Am Love," or "I Am That I Am." To connect with the Christ and I Am angels and feel their consciousness and power is exalting and transformative.

The goal of all of the angels of each of our bodies is to fulfill the divine purpose of our God Self. For the Being we call Earth, as well as for the Being that is each of us, this simply means the complete and perfect functioning of Nature, of all of Nature. All of the angels of your own life stream of identity and those of your patient may be accessed for healing.

HOW TO USE THE ANGELS FOR HEALING:

1. Open your heart with love and trust to the angels of your own or your patient's I Am, Christ, or soul's body. Trust is important, for the angels will not adapt to your techniques. Your techniques must follow them! Your success will reflect how well you can follow Nature.

2. Close your eyes. Picture the body and locate its problem on the screen of your heart. Share with the angels the problem you are concerned with, for instance, a dairy allergy that gives sinus congestion, or ankle pain. The more specific the problem, the more specific the angels you will call forth. Start with an open mind, so that the angels can give you an overview of the case. They may show you something that at first doesn't make sense, but you will soon be surprised at its wisdom.

3. Ask for a vision of how the angels of the body would like to heal this problem. You may be very adept at this immediately, or it may take some practice. Remember your level of consciousness determines where you get answers. You will get a vision that powerfully magnetizes the necessary angels to work. This understanding will also magnetize your hands, your mind, and your energy bodies to speak the right words, to place your hands exactly where necessary, and to bring the perfect energy into the body to help remove the blockages or integrate the light that has already entered.

4. Ask where to start. Follow the angels' lead. The angels heal in waves that touch all the subtle bodies. We must respect the order in which the patient's angels want the care to be given. Keep asking questions. You will be shown how the healing will best unfold. You may be shown by feeling in your own body the next area to work on. This does *not* mean you are drawing the problem into yourself to transmute. Let the angels take care of it all. Your body just resonates with the healing and you get some healing, too.

5. Once you have opened the doors, ask the angels what kind

of support would help: nutritional therapies, specific exercises, rest, laughter, music, visualization, breathing, tones of color. We no longer need to do everything ourselves; angels are here to help. We cannot afford to believe that we know best. We have a partnership with the angels that can make earth a paradise once again. Let go of all the pictures you have stored of how you should be healed. Let Nature nurture you with joy.

The above contribution was excerpted with kind permission of the author from *Connecting Links,* vol. 1, no. 3. Dr. Linda Zwingeberg Fickes resides in Hawaii with her daughter and husband, Bob. Linda and Bob offer courses and seminars around the country. You may call them at (808) 262-7239 or contact them by writing:

> Council of Light, Inc.
> 1496 Humu'ula St.
> Kailua, HI 96734

El Shaddai — The God Who Is More Than Enough
by Daniel Kaufman

The Sufis have a wonderful word for God — El Shaddai, which means "the God Who Is More Than Enough."

El Shaddai is my favorite term for expressing unlimited blessings bestowed upon those willing to receive, the love that is heaped upon us if we are loving and willing to receive love, the bounteous beauty of the angelic world, and the exquisite beauty of our own earthly paradise if we are willing to experience it.

I have always felt that gratitude is the key to releasing any painful and stuck moments of self-pity. At such times, I ask my angels and guardians of gratitude to remind me of the numerous blessings in my life. It is impossible to indulge in self-pity when I remember that I have eyes that see, hands that can touch and paint and write, a mouth to kiss my beloved wife and baby, a brain to enjoy life (and to create problems to resolve), a heart that pumps millions of times automatically, and the ability to feel love. These blessings reflect the generosity of El Shaddai — that I should have such blessings, and also angels to help me, and friends and air and water, that for no other reason than my seemingly random birth on May 4th, 1949, in New York City, amidst millions of other randomly born others, I should have so many ways to find pleasure and love and fulfillment in a land of freedom and opportunity.

This is *more than enough*; this is the infinite love and benevolence of the Creator, of the Universal Principle — that I was born with the capacity to know myself, to find within myself the same beauty that I perceive in the outer world.

Two things inspire me to awe: the starry heavens above and the moral universe within.

Albert Einstein

This, again, is the generosity of El Shaddai, the God Who Is More Than Enough. And gratitude for this generosity of abundance and guidance (just remember to *ask* for it!) will heal untold frustrations and misery.

My favorite Jewish song is another exquisite reminder of El Shaddai — the God Who Is More Than Enough. On Passover (a most holy holiday celebrating the Jews' escape from slavery), we sing "Dayenu," which translates, depending on which Hagadah you look at, as "It would have been enough" or (in another translation) "We should have been more grateful." The song tells the story of all the miracles one after the next that made possible the Jews' escape from Egypt and their subsequent miraculous survival in the desert for forty years. After each miracle (the parting of the Red Sea, the appearance of food to feed them in the desert, being led into Israel, the land of freedom), the refrain "Dayenu" is repeated: "It would have been enough."

So, when my angels don't give me all the guidance I expect or demand, I back down and say to them, "Okay, you've been really generous already. If you'd just given me my life and not my wife or my wife and not my baby or my baby and not my health or my health and not my talent: Dayenu." It would have been enough; for any one of these gifts, I should be grateful.

And usually if the gratitude is sufficient and sincere, my angelic guardians (or whoever is showing me the way) will give me a new gift (if I am paying attention) as a bonus for saluting the God Who Is More Than Enough.

Dolphins and Angels With Kutira and Moonjay

The very day I was wondering about the connection between dolphins and angels, Kutira Decosterd showed up to shed light on the subject.

Kutira's life path is very much that of a human angel. One of the goals of her lifework is to help individuals cross personal boundaries that limit creativity and to help generate a more playful, rewarding way of life. A Tantric Yoga teacher for many years, she has found a way to combine this ancient practice of energy-raising with her interest in dolphins and whales, by creating Oceanic Tantra.

In one of the guided images she uses, Kutira takes people into the sea to meet a dolphin. You find yourself hanging onto the dolphin, and as you get used to the rhythms of the sea through breathing and relaxation you find you are now in a spiral motion with your dolphin. As the motion increases, you have been catapulted into space, flying with your dolphin into the realms of heaven, where time and space vanish and there is only freedom. Now the dolphin has become your guardian angel. When you are ready to come back to the earth plane, you ask your guardian dolphin for a gift to keep from the journey. Many beautiful gifts are bestowed on people in this way. One individual received a glowing crystal from her dolphin, which the dolphin then planted in her heart forever.

Kutira once took a video tape of dolphins dancing and swimming in their water ballet style and superimposed it on a video tape of a beautiful sky filled with magnificent clouds. It was at this moment that she felt the connection between dolphins and angels. Watching the dolphins flying and dancing in the clouds transported her into a realm where all life connects.

Kutira and her partner Moonjay gave me these insights into the ways dolphins are like angels—the angels of the sea:

> Dolphins inspire play and laughter.
> Dolphins can be used as a connection with a higher consciousness—a special state of being which they seem to carry around with them, and which they seem to open up for humans in their presence.
> Hawaiian mythology traces dolphins' origins from the stars in the heavens.
> Dolphins are known to be helpful to humans in distress at sea.
> Dolphins don't take things seriously; their field of gravity is lighter.
> Dolphins awaken the child within us; they open us to our playful self.
> Dolphins and children connect easily and naturally.
> When people see dolphins, their mood is lightened and a sense of joy, excitement, and love prevails.

The connection between dolphins and angels is definitely worth exploring. I'm convinced that the dolphins have a message for our species and that it is similar to the message angels have for us: Lighten up and play more!

If you would like to find out more about the wonderful things Kutira and Moonjay are doing, contact them at:

Kahula Hawaiian Institute for Inner Transformation
P.O. Box 1747
Mahawao, Maui, HI 96768

An Afternoon With Suzanna Solomon

Looking through a section of the local Malibu newspaper, I found the following ad listed under "Announcements": "You are not alone — your guardian angels are all around you. They want to love you, source you, inspire you, counsel you in all you are and do. If you are ready to go beyond your known reality, then come with me on a wondrous journey and meet with your angels. Suzanna."

I cut out the ad, and set it aside in a place where I would see it from time to time. A few weeks passed and spontaneously I called Suzanna. She was warmly receptive and agreed to let me come and talk to her about angels, with the possibility of writing about it for my book.

When I walked into her apartment, I immediately felt a strong presence of angels. Suzanna took me on a tour of her apartment, which looked and felt like it could be heaven. The colors I always associate with heaven were in every room, displayed in true artist's fashion. I noticed that Suzanna collected rocks, pebbles, and gemstones, and that they were displayed in each room. This was particularly exciting to me because I, too, have rocks, gemstones, and pebbles displayed throughout my living space. I asked what all these rocks could mean and she told me, "They represent the earth realm in which we live, the realm in which we can be in touch with the devic kingdom. The rocks also provide grounding for the incredible lightness of being that comes from being in close contact with the angels."

Suzanna has seven angels who come to her, and she has drawn beautiful portraits of these angels. Each angel has brought a profound experience her way, which she is going to put together with the portraits in a book she is creating.

Suzanna has helped hundreds of people connect with their guardian angels. She does this by taking people into an "altered state." To make sure that the beings who come are angels, Suzanna tests each entity. Some of the tests she uses (she says there are many) are basic questions such as "Are you from the angelic realm?" After that, she told me, "If the beings/entities are not from the angelic realm, they usually disappear, or the feeling of their presence leaves." Other questions include: "Are you here to give the experience of the God-self?" "Do you come for my highest spiritual good?" "Are you from the Christ vibration?" "Are you of the Love vibration?"

If angels are around, the person will get an incredible feeling of lovingness and lightness. Suzanna agreed with me that angels are full of humor and light. They are very funny beings. If an entity comes who is heavy and serious, she knows that that entity is not of the angelic realm.

Suzanna told me that some of the people she has helped connect with their angels have had the most amazing experiences, like cosmic consciousness expansions; then, six months later, they were right back with all the craziness in their life just the way it was before. The reason this happens, she explained, is that "they don't listen, they won't ask, and they don't do the meditations. To stay with the higher vibration, you must ask for the connection. The angels will not push you over: If you don't shift your vibration and raise it to their level, life will not change at all. Guardian angels are always around us, but only when we truly *acknowledge* and *ask* and *have faith* will they come to source the vibrations of our higher self." She added an analogy to electricity: "If you don't stick the cord into the plug, nothing happens. The electricity is there, but you have to connect with it; you have to turn on the switch for it to be any use to you. Guardian angels come to us in many ways to teach us. When we can allow that and stay awake our life will change."

Suzanna asked her guardian angels if maybe it wasn't the right time for these people to meet their own guardians. Her angels told her that the time was right to introduce them but that the people were not ready to change their lives just yet.

Connecting children and teens with their guardian angels is an especially rewarding experience. Some of the children Suzanna has worked with have readily seen and talked to angels and fairies since they can first remember. The father of such a child who had contact with the fairy world thought it would be interesting to see if this same connection could happen with the child's angels. So he brought the child to Suzanna. The connection was powerful because the child already accepted the world of angels and was ready to meet them.

Meeting their angels through Suzanna's guidance brings many positive changes to many people's lives, and lets them know they are not alone. If you would like more information about Suzanna, contact her at:

>Suzanna Solomon
>c/o Terry Taylor
>P.O. Box 6847
>Malibu, CA 90265

Animal Angels
by Nancy Grimley Carleton

My pet rabbit Willow is an angel. I'm convinced of it. At 2.7 pounds, he is a furry bundle of unconditional love. Willow has been my rabbit, and I have been his person, for three years now. And from the first time I saw him, he has filled my heart with lightness and love. Even in my most serious moods, when I see Willow come hopping into the room something inside of me opens up and I am overcome with gratitude and joy. No matter how I'm feeling, no matter what I'm going through, he is there as a steady source of acceptance and love. In the evenings, I get into bed and lie with him directly over my heart. His body sinks trustingly into mine, we breathe together, and both of us experience a piece of heaven.

I believe that many treasured pets are angels in disguise. Angels know that sometimes we humans need the comfort and warmth of flesh and blood. An angel came to me when I was five years old and desperately in need of a positive connection to life. She took the form of Tippy, a small black dog with white paws, white chest and nose, and a white tip on her tail. We owned her mother, Lucky, another probable angel, who gave birth to her puppies on our couch (a big mess, as I wrote in a kindergarten account of the event). I watched Tippy being born, and I knew from the moment I saw her that she had come to be my dog. She was the first of the three puppies to wag her tail, and for several weeks she wagged it only for me. She made me feel special and loved. My mother let us keep her (we could only keep one of the puppies) and for the next sixteen years, until I was twenty-one, she was my faithful and loving companion. We spent hours playing together; she had more patience than any other dog I've known, even allowing me to dress her in clothes (I seldom played with dolls). At night and in the mornings, she cuddled warmly with me whether I was sad or angry, happy or depressed. Tippy gave me many gifts, but foremost among them was unconditional love and acceptance. I will never forget her.

Today I opened the mail to a letter from Mary Kay Wright-Malear, a bodyworker in the Bay Area who has held two raffles in the past couple of years to raise funds for treatments for her much-loved dog, Brujo. The letter informed those of us who had contributed to the raffle that Brujo had died in July: "He was my best friend," read the card Mary Kay had printed in his memory. She also included a quotation from Meher Baba, which captures very clearly the quality of love animal angels can give: "Love is essentially self-communicative. Those who do not have it catch it from those who have it. True Love is unconquerable and irresistible and it goes on gathering power and spreading itself until it transforms everyone whom it touches." The love and acceptance pets give the people around them doesn't end there; it fills us with the kind of love that spreads out to touch others.

To close, I'd like to share a synchronistic experience I had regarding animals as angels. Last Christmas, two of my psychotherapy clients who know each other gave me a gift. Both of them knew I liked rabbits (my favorite pair of earrings are dangling golden rabbits), though neither of them knew of my interest in angels. But the gift they gave me was perfect. It was a porcelain Christmas tree ornament in the shape of a white rabbit's head and ears with angel's wings sprouting out the shoulders. It now hangs over Willow's hutch, keeping watch over him and reminding me every day that angels can take many forms.

Nancy Grimley Carleton, M.A., in addition to being the editor of this book, works as a transpersonal therapist (M.F.C.C. Reg. Intern #IMF 12548) under the supervision of Kathleen C. Tamm, licensed Marriage Family Child Counselor. Nancy is particularly interested in helping clients who are grieving the loss of animal friends, many of whom are angels. She can be reached at:

Nancy Grimley Carleton
Blue Oak Therapy Center
2034 Blake Street, Suite 5
Berkeley, CA 94704
(415) 649-9818

John Lilly's Dog
by Francis Jeffrey

John Lilly, the famous neurophysiologist and dolphin researcher, tells several stories about childhood encounters with angels, whom he sometimes calls Guardians, or Beings. Here, his first such meeting is described:

Once, as a tot, he had nearly stumbled off a cliff. Ja mey, the family dog, grabbed little John and pulled him from the brink. John did not realize that Ja mey had just saved his life. He felt a flash of anger against the dog for tearing his jacket and pinching his shoulder in its canine teeth. At that point, the Guardian appeared to set things right. "You shouldn't be angry at Ja mey," explained the Being, "because I made him pull you back from the brink. I did it to save your body from being badly damaged by the fall."

His relationship with the Being would continue. Somehow it was attached to him, was perhaps inside him, perhaps part of himself.

This passage is excerpted with kind permission from *John Lilly, So Far . . .* (the biography of Dr. John C. Lilly) by Francis Jeffrey (Los Angeles: J. P. Tarcher, Inc./St. Martin's Press, 1989).

John Lilly and His Guardian Beings
as told to Terry Taylor

From the age of three to the age of eight, John C. Lilly had two constant companions. They were his guardian angels. The companions were very beautiful, with huge white wings and blond hair. It was impossible to tell if they were male or female. The angels' huge white wings were a blessing on hot days; it was nice to have them near because they would fan John. They never took him up for a flight, but that was only because John was afraid to go.

When John was seven, the angels told him they would take him to church to show him a vision of Christ, the saints, God, and Mary. Soon it happened: There he was in the midst of thousands of singing angels praising God. John felt the radiance of love, and he was very moved.

After the vision, John thanked the angels, and they told him not to tell anyone what he had seen. But he made the mistake of telling a nun at school. She looked extremely surprised, then scolded John, telling him that only saints had visions and that he should not lie. John took this to mean that he wasn't a saint, so he must have done something illegal. After this altercation, the angels told him that when he was older he would know just how much of the experience he could write and talk about, and when it was safe to do so.

When John was eight, the two angels finally went into his head, so no one else would be bothered by them.

John's guardians saved his life many times, so many times, in fact, that John says it's astonishing to him. Some children have only one guardian angel, but John had two, and, if you know anything about his life, he certainly needed two. Later in life, John referred to them as the Beings, and he wrote about them in many of his books.

John told me that, when I am older, I will find that angels are tougher than I think. John discovered that his angels, or Beings as he later called them, were actually a part of ECCO. ECCO stands for Earth Coincidence Control Office, and angels act as agents of ECCO (or vice versa) to arrange coincidences for humans on earth. (ECCO agents teach their lessons whether you like them or not.) The structure of ECCO is very intricate and involved. It is discussed in the new biography of John, *John Lilly, So Far . . .* by Francis Jeffrey (listed in the bibliography). If you would like to know more about John and ECCO, and more about John's many experiences with his angelic Beings, this would be a good book to read.

Karin Jensen and the Japanese Angels

It all started during a meditation. Karin, sitting in a circle of crystals with a clay mask on her face, was having a powerful experience. To encourage her interest in drawing, her son had just given her a sketchbook, which was at her side. She picked up the sketchbook, and a mysterious force came through her. She started drawing designs that had a Japanese look and feel to them. These designs flowed out through her hand, quickly filling each page. Karin realized she was channeling some source outside herself.

The designs always started in the lower right-hand corner of the page. At first, the channeling activity took a lot of Karin's energy, and she would be very tired afterward. But as she went along, she worked out a way to handle the energy drain, streamlining her body's response to the signals flowing through her, until she actually began to gain energy from the process. Now she looks forward to channeling the designs as an energizing meditation. And she has since accumulated a huge collection of these calligraphic pages.

Many people have seen the designs, and some of these people have had powerful reactions. A dancer friend of Karin's went wild over the designs and said they were truly a dance on paper; she had the same feeling from looking at the designs that she got when dancing. The designs convey a feeling that removes her from the gravity of the earth plane. My own first reaction to seeing them was that each little design is the dance of a different angel.

Through a series of coincidences, a woman named Elizabeth came to the town where Karin lives to do a ceremony involving angels who appear to people in Peru. She saw Karin's drawings and knew she must take them to Peru with her, to show a Peruvian sage who calls on angels to materialize. (The angels usually oblige.) Back in Peru, Elizabeth met some of these angels and showed them Karin's drawings, and in a letter to Karin she wrote, "The first day I went, the angels looked at your pages of writing and immediately said that it is the ancient sacred writing of Japanese angels. It is actually sacred prayers." The angels want Karin to travel to Peru so that they can translate the prayers to her in person.

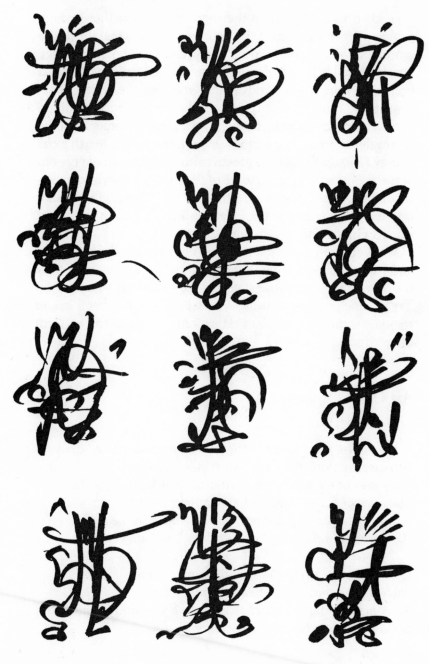

Elizabeth says that when the angels materialize they first appear as a powerful wind at the point where one's feet touch the ground, or at the point where one's hands are holding a large quartz crystal ball. This energy forms into a flurry of wings, and then the entire angel stands before you. For the angels to appear, there must be plenty of crystals around, purportedly to conduct the electromagnetic energy they need in order to clothe themselves in tangible form. (Or perhaps it's the earth's *ch'i* energy.) Elizabeth says the process also takes a lot of energy out of the people in the group; some of their energy goes into materializing the angels. One interesting connection with the crystals is that crystals were present in large quantities when Karin first started channeling her drawings.

Many interesting happenings revolve around the drawings, and Karin feels it is time that they go out in the world. Study the drawings in a receptive state and see what you come up with. Try channeling some drawings yourself; allow whatever is in you to come out onto paper as a dance of life. This is truly a form of spiritual art therapy.

An Ode to Angels
by Alice Way

Angels bring good tidings of hope and joy and peace,
But also comfort when our spirits need release.
They also bring us visions in luminescent light—
Messages of forgiveness that stay forever bright;
A word, a name, a fragrance, or voices that we hear,
We do not always need these signs to know they're near.

Often they are using the skill of human hands,
And human prayers uplifted over many lands.
They help us make hard choices or help us courage find,
Or give us opportunities to be more kind.

We thank our guardian angels for their faithful care,
And for the ways that humankind can learn to share.

Whate'er our name for angels or what our name for God,
The network of the spirit pervades our earthly sod.
So let us join the angels in their joyful songs,
Never, though, forgetting to help to right the wrongs.

Alice Way was a Quaker educator who founded Pacific Oaks
College and the Ackworth Friends Elementary School in Pasa-
dena, California. For forty-seven years, she was codirector of
these schools, involving herself most extensively in special education; she never gave up on a child however difficult the case.
Her guiding light was giving compassionately to others. Visitors
to her house often noticed heavenly scents. Alice would explain,
"That just means the angels are back." She wrote "An Ode to
Angels" on Christmas day, 1986. She died in mid-1989, in her
late seventies, after a lifetime of service.

The Mount Shasta Angel
by Thomas LeRose

On Friday, August 14, 1978, at about 11:00 P.M. in Mount Shasta,
California, an angel appeared on a television screen. The television set belonged to a local resident, Ms. Boettcher. She had
turned on her T.V. hoping to catch an update on the events
surrounding the harmonic convergence, when the angel suddenly appeared. The angel emerged as a blast of light, super-
imposing itself over normal cable programming.

Saturday, as word-of-mouth reports went out, Ms. Boettcher's
house was filled with a steady stream of visitors. With each
passing day, as more people believed in the angel, the image
grew clearer.

A T.V. repairman was called out to examine the set, but he

couldn't find anything wrong with it. A video engineer also examined the set and was convinced that the angel was not a trick image. He concurred with both a T.V. repairman and a nuclear physicist who came to the house that "there is no explanation in terms of nature as we know it" (from the *Mount Shasta Herald,* Wednesday, August 19, 1987). Other T.V. sets were brought into the house, but they could not produce the image. The first set was relocated, and still the image remained.

The angel manifested itself on a T.V. screen to demonstrate "the birth of heaven on earth." This angel is a rainbow being of light with a pinkish-white heart center. It stands in a star position encircled by a golden halo. The angel has appeared to awaken the angel within our own hearts. Angels offer us unconditional love and are waiting to guide us homeward.

"Yes, dear ones, let it be known that the angels are truly here on earth!" received by Solara.

For further information on the Mount Shasta angel, contact Thomas LeRose, who photographed it during its appearance.

Thomas LeRose
P.O. Box 72A
El Portal, CA 95318

Other Comments on Angels

The following is contributed by Linda Hayden: "Angels can appear when a person's body is very ill. Usually they don't say much. Sometimes they do. A rebirth experience follows."

A letter I received, from an angelic being named Filomena stated: "I am an Angel. My purpose is to reveal the flame of light that I am, and to enlighten you with the sheer innocent delight of expressing the I am in my physical body. In my personal process of integrating body, heart, and soul, I'm revealing what I see and feel. I'm balancing out the seeking of my own wonder."

My friend Shannon Boomer asked her son Gideon to tell us what he thought angels were. He answered, "Oh, they're just plain old air!"

Quotations About Angels

Angels are aspects of God that touch us in mysterious and subtle ways and on many levels of the mind. They are divine messengers of God that can transform our attitudes, change our thought patterns and renew our ideals if we open ourselves to their heedings.

Harvey Humann

Though angels are both the messengers and the message of God, that makes them no easier to receive. For one thing, we almost never recognize them, even when they knock at our door.

F. Forrester Church

It is not because Angels are holier than men or devils that makes them Angels, but because they do not expect holiness from one another, but from God alone.

William Blake

Millions of spiritual creatures walk the earth unseen, both when we sleep and when we wake.

Milton

I throw my selfe downe in my Chamber, and I call in and invite God, and his Angels thither, and when they are there,

I neglect God and his Angels, for the noise of a Flie, for the rattling of a Coach, for the whining of a doore.

John Donne

Silently one by one, in the infinite meadows of Heaven, Blossomed the lovely stars, the forget-me-nots of the Angels

H.W. Longfellow

Chapter 36

Noteworthy
Angel Progaganda

Angel Bits and Glossary

GALLUP POLLS

According to the Gallup poll in 1978, *A Surprising Number of Americans Believe in Paranormal Phenomena*, a majority of fifty-four percent believe in angels, increasing to sixty-eight percent among people whose religious beliefs are important to them. The study found that those who believe in supernatural beings are generally younger and better educated.

According to the Gallup poll in 1988, *Teen Belief in Angels Is on the Rise*, more teens than ever believe in angels. Three teens in four believe in angels, or seventy-four percent nationwide.

GLOSSARY

Ange passe: This is French for "angel passing." When there is a lull or quieting in a conversation, the French say, "ange passe," because the quiet means an angel has passed overhead.

Angel satchel: This is a term coined by Mary Beth Crain for a place to put unwanted energy and personalities that are interfering in your life. The angels will pick it up for you and send it far away (possibly all the way to the planet Pluto).

Kairos: A moment of God's grace in which angels do their thing—an opportune time when conditions are right for the accomplishment of a crucial action. A decisive action.

AFFIRMATION OF ARCHANGEL MICHAEL:

Divine light of the highest order under the protection of the archangel Michael. [Repeat this three times for protection in any situation.]

THEMES AND SYMBOLS SURROUNDING ANGELS

Angels are often portrayed in portraits surrounded by the following symbols:

> The lily flower: symbolizes purity
> Bearing a palm: symbolizes victory
> Musical instrument: symbolizes praise
> Trumpet: the voice of God
> Carrying a thurible (an incense burner): symbolizes adoration and prayer
> Pilgrim's staff: symbolizes readiness
> Wings: symbolize the speed and quickness with which they fulfill the divine command
> Nimbus (plural, nimbi): refers to a bright cloud surrounding deities when they appear on earth—an aura that spiritual beings from the heaven plane have around them
> Halo: the holy shining light that encircles an angel's head; the light streaming from the head
> Aureola: the full aura of light outlining a person or angel
> The glory: a combination of both the halo and aura
> Diadem: a crown or headband symbolizing royal authority

ORDERS OF ANGELS

There are three orders of angels, each consisting of three choirs, making a total of nine choirs of angels.

Those closest to God

1. **The seraphim:** Purifying and enlightened powers, shown with six wings and flames of fire around them, they are led by Uriel and call out to one another the words: "Holy, Holy, Holy is the Lord of hosts" (see Isaiah 6:3).
2. **The cherubim:** With the power of knowing, they are shown with multieyed peacock's feathers symbolizing their all-knowing power. Their leader is Jophiel.
3. **The thrones:** With the simplicity from purification, they are shown as wheels of fire, the throne bearers of God, representing divine majesty. Their leader is Japhkiel.

Priest-princes of the court of heaven

4. **The dominions or dominations:** Aspiring to true lordship, they carry the scepter and sword to symbolize the divine power over all creation. Their leader is Zadkiel.
5. **The virtues or authorities:** Powerful assimilations of the will of God, they carry out the instruments of the passion of Christ. Their leader is Haniel.
6. **The powers:** Orderly authorities, they carry flaming swords to protect humankind. Their leader is Raphael.

The ministering angels

7. **The principalities:** Princely powers, they watch over the leaders of people, carrying scepters and crosses. Their leader is Chamael.
8. **The archangels:** Leaders among angels, their leader is Michael.
9. **The angels:** Beings of light who reveal the divine mysteries and who don't have special ranks or commissions in the celestial army.

WELL-KNOWN ANGELS FOR HELP OR INSPIRATION

Raphael

Hebrew *Rapha'* (to heal) and *'el* (God): God has healed

Raphael means God heals or divine healer

Leader of the powers

He is charged with healing the earth, and through him the earth furnishes an abode for humans, whom he also heals

Healing and mercy: He directs spiritual beams into hospitals, institutions, and homes where his healing beams are needed

Intellect, curiosity, and instruction in the sciences

Guardian and treasurer of creative talents

Symbol: a sword or an arrow that has been well sharpened

He carries a golden vial of balm

Time of day: the dawn

Season and colors: spring; soft greens and all tints of blue

Bible story: Tobias

Michael

Hebrew *Mikha'el* means "Who is God?" His name is a battle cry

Captain of the heavenly host, leader of the archangels, viceroy of heaven

Also known as St. Michael

The lord of the way

The slayer of the dragon of evil intentions

Guardian of holy places

Ruler of the fourth heaven

Often equated with the Holy Ghost

Midday angel clad in armor, with shield and weapon

Fights first Satan and his demons, then all the enemies of God's own people

Known as an angel who cleanses persons, groups, or localities of discord and evil

Represents the right, the creative, that which should be done

The master of the energy of balance

Element: fire, purification, perfection

Season and colors: summer; deep green, vivid blues, golden, and rose red

Invoked as a champion against all adversity and when you need courage and a strong defender; success

Day: Sunday

The sun

Direction to invoke: south

Red candle

Gabriel

Hebrew *gebher* means "man and el," or God

Gabriel means man of God or strength of God

Bible: announcing of Jesus to the Virgin Mary, and through the prophet Daniel

Presides over paradise

Sits on the left-hand side of God

Associated with a trumpet, symbolizing the voice of God

Usually portrayed as carrying a lily, olive branch, or torch

Bringer of good news and maker of changes

Annunciation, resurrection, mercy, truth

The potency of God

Procreation and resurrection

Love is his great force factor

Late afternoon; peaceful vibration

Fluidlike activity, water

Autumn; tans, browns, dark greens

Invoked toward the west

Favorite day: Monday

Important figure in Muslim religion: the guardian angel of the prophet Mohammed

Inspired Joan of Arc to help the king of France

Uriel

Hebrew: fire of God

Angel of prophecy who inspires and conveys ideas to writer and teachers

The angel of interpretation and salvation

Shown with a scroll as his symbol

Leader of the seraphim

The alchemist imparting transforming ideas for the realization of goals (especially those of the discouraged and weak)

Angel of the month of September

Associated with the arts, with music in particular

Haniel

Glory or grace of God

All powers of love

Governor of Venus

Invoked as power against evil

Angel of the month of December

Metatron

King of angels

Prince of the divine face

Charged with the sustenance of mankind

Link between the human and divine

Tallest angel in heaven

Resides in seventh heaven (the dwelling place of God)

Highest power of abundance

When invoked, he can appear as a pillar of fire, his face more dazzling than the sun

Raziel

Secret of God

Angel of the mysteries

Knowledge; guardian of originality

Habitat Chokmah, the realm of pure ideas

Auriel

> Angel of night
> Associated with the earth
> Winter: he is the creative force in the ebb period
> The seed is in the earth and all is dark
> Helps us contemplate the future
> Winter colors: black, brown, gray

In brief

> **Michael:** courage, strong defense, divine protection, shield and sword
> **Gabriel:** bringer of news, maker of changes, trumpet
> **Haniel:** all powers of love
> **Raphael:** God has healed, golden vial of balm
> **Uriel:** emergencies, judgment, scroll
> **Raziel:** knowledge, guardian of originality, habitat Chokmah, the realm of pure ideas
> **Camael:** power in interpersonal relationships, self-discipline
> **Metatron:** highest power of abundance, chancellor of heaven

Annotated Bibliography

BOOKS OF GENERAL ANGEL INFORMATION

Adler, Mortimer J. *The Angels and Us.* New York: Macmillan Publishing Co., Inc., 1982.
Written by a prolific contemporary philosopher/thinker, this book contains original thinking, artfully addressing the age-old questions about angels.

Church, F. Forrester. *Entertaining Angels: A Guide to Heaven for Atheists and True Believers.* San Francisco: Harper and Row, 1987.
Very fun and thought provoking. An honest look at heaven, including the paradoxical nature of the Christian viewpoint

on heaven. Lots of humorous scenarios. Contains true angelic insight.

D'Angelo, Dorie. *Living With Angels*. Carmel, CA: First Church of Angels, 1980.

Written by a human angel with simple angelic wisdom and true angel stories. Inspirational. Includes some methods for contacting angels.

Davidson, Gustav. *A Dictionary of Angels (Including the Fallen Angels)*. New York: The Free Press, 1971.

One of the most bizarre and amazing compilations of data on angels. It had to have taken a lifetime to collect all the information. An angel archive, dictionary style.

Gilmore, G. Don. *Angels, Angels, Everywhere*. New York: Pilgrim Press, 1981.

Contains historical perceptions of angels, from the world's great religions and cultures, and describes the various forms angels have taken and their roles in history. Real-life accounts of experiences with angels, including some well-known personalities.

Graham, Billy. *Angels: God's Secret Agents*. Waco, TX: Word Books, 1986.

Angels are discussed as "spiritual creatures created by God for the service of Christendom and the church." Based on accounts from the Bible.

Hodson, Geoffrey. *The Brotherhood of Angels and Men*. Wheaton, IL: Theosophical Publishing House, 1982.

Written by a clairvoyant, this book consists of messages he received direct from the angelic kingdom.

Humann, Harvey. *The Many Faces of Angels*. Marina del Rey, CA: DeVorss and Co., 1986.

Described as an introduction or overview on the subject of angels, from a metaphysical standpoint. The author is quite a wordsmith and conveys the beauty and essence of angels in a fitting way.

MacGregor, Geddes. *Angels: Ministers of Grace*. New York: Paragon House, 1988.

The author is a theologian and philosopher. The book is scholarly, confronting the age-old questions about angels. Examines the role of angels in art (contains about forty illustrations), music, mythology, and the Bible. Very complete compared to other books of its kind.

Moolenburgh, H.C. *A Handbook of Angels.* Great Britain: C.W. Daniel Co. Ltd., 1984.
A very interesting book written by a Dutch medical doctor, who started his own survey by asking patients about their experiences with angels. Ahead of its time in many ways.

Parente, Fr. Pascal P. *Beyond Space: A Book About the Angels.* Rockford, IL: Tan Books and Publishers, Inc., 1973.
Catholic viewpoint and references, mostly dealing with angelic hierarchy.

Ronner, John. *Do You Have a Guardian Angel?* Indialantic, FL: Mamre Press, Inc., 1985.
Answers to eighty-three questions on angels, imparting interesting folklore and age-old wisdom, along with current interest and information.

Solara. *Invoking Your Celestial Guardians.* Mt. Shasta, CA: Star-Borne Unlimited, 1988.
A book written by someone who has passed the boundary and connected with a deeply spiritual order of angels. Tells people how to find their true angel names and rediscover the angels they are.

BOOKS ABOUT THE DEVIC KINGDOM

Bloom, William. *Devas, Fairies and Angels (A Modern Approach).* Somerset, England: Gothic Image Publications, 1986.
Short pamphlet; contains a lot of insightful information.

Maclean, Dorothy. *To Hear the Angels Sing.* Issaquah, WA: Lorian Press, 1987.
This is my personal favorite of all angel books. It is inspiring and contains actual messages recorded from the angels. After reading it, you get a real sense of who and what angels are,

and what your connection to nature is, and how important the devic kingdom is.

Newhouse, Flower A. *Rediscovering the Angels and Natives of Eternity.* Escondido, CA: The Christwatch Ministry, 1976.
Written by a Christian mystic who set out to bring angels back into Christian teaching. Covers a wide range of mystical angel information, with emphasis on the devic kingdom.

BOOKS FOR "SENSITIVES" AND SEEKERS

Bowers, Barbara. *What Color Is Your Aura?* New York: Pocket Books, 1989.
This book includes a test that not only tells you the color of your aura but also gives you tremendous insight into your personality when you read about the color or colors in your aura.

Calhoun, Marcy. *Are You Really Too Sensitive?* Nevada City, CA: Blue Dolphin Press, Inc., 1987.
Sensitives need to understand themselves, so that they won't think that something is wrong or vastly different about them. This book is written to help the true sensitive in all aspects of his or her life—from money to love.

Fields, Rick. *Chop Wood, Carry Water.* Los Angeles: Jeremy P. Tarcher, Inc., 1984.
A book you probably either own or have seen in your favorite bookstore. A very valuable handbook for spiritual seekers regardless of their level of awareness or stage.

Roman, Sanaya. *Spiritual Growth.* Tiburon, CA: H.J. Kramer, Inc., 1989.
This is the best book I know for understanding your higher self, and developing ways to *become* your higher self in your everyday life.

PROSPERITY AND ABUNDANCE

Ponder, Catherine. *The Prospering Power of Love.* Marina del Rey, CA: Devorss and Co., 1966.
Has a great section about writing to angels.

Roman, Sanaya, and Packer, Duane. *Creating Money.* Tiburon, CA: H.J. Kramer, Inc., 1988.
By far the most complete book on abundance and prosperity. Many helpful techniques, affirmations, and exercises are included that are known to produce results.

HUMOR AND HEALING

Cousins, Norman. *The Anatomy of an Illness as Perceived by the Patient.* New York: Norton, 1979.
This famous journalist was stricken with a mysterious inflammatory and degenerative illness, which doctors were at a loss to treat. He cured himself through a program of laughter, in a nonstressful environment.

Samra, Cal. *The Joyful Christ: The Healing Power of Humor.* San Francisco: Harper and Row, 1985.
A study of humor in the Bible—holy humor. Also looks at joy and humor as the true healing powers the universe (God) provides.

Works Cited Bibliography

In the interest of maintaining the light tone of this book, I did not want to weigh you down with extensive footnotes in the text. This bibliography will enable you to track down the sources for most of the quotations cited in the book. Some of the titles included here are described briefly in the Annotated Bibliography in Part Five.

Addison, Joseph. "The Spectator." Cited in John Bartlett (Ed.) *Bartlett's Quotations*. Boston: Little, Brown and Co., 1955, p. 326.

Blake, William. "I am not ashamed . . ." Cited in Harvey Humann, *The Many Faces of Angels*. Marina del Rey, CA: DeVorss and Co., 1986, p. 27.

Blake, William. "The Angel That Presided." Cited in John Bartlett (Ed.), *Bartlett's Quotations*. Boston: Little, Brown and Co., 1955, p. 407.

Blake, William. "It is not because Angels are holier . . ." Cited in Carroll E. Simcox, *A Treasury of Quotations on Christian Themes*. New York: Crossroad, 1975, p. 37.

Bucher, Steve. Personal communication, 1989.

Chesterton, G.K. *Orthodoxy*. Garden City, NY: Image, 1959, p. 120.

Church, F. Forrester. *Entertaining Angels: A Guide to Heaven for Atheists and True Believers*. San Francisco: Harper and Row, 1987.

Cousins, Norman. *The Anatomy of an Illness as Perceived by the Patient*. New York: Norton, 1979.

D'Angelo, Dorie. *Living With Angels*. Carmel, CA: First Church of Angels, 1980, p. 48.

Davidson, Gustav. *A Dictionary of Angels (Including the Fallen Angels)*. New York: The Free Press, 1971, p. 176.

Donne, John. "Sermons." Cited in John Bartlett (Ed.), *Bartlett's Quotations*. Boston: Little, Brown and Co., 1955, p. 255.

Fields, Rick. *Chop Wood, Carry Water*. Los Angeles: Jeremy P. Tarcher, Inc., 1984, p. 192.

Fox, Emmet. Cited in Catherine Ponder, *The Prospering Power of Love*. Marina de Rey, CA: DeVorss and Co., 1966, p. 49.

Frank, Anne. Cited in John Bartlett (Ed.), *Bartlett's Quotations*. Boston: Little, Brown and Co., 1955, p. 909.

Gallup, Alec, and Gallup, George, Jr. *Teen Belief in Angels Is on the Rise*. Princeton, NJ: Gallup Poll, 1988.

Gallup, George. *A Surprising Number of Americans Believe in Paranormal Phenomena*. Princeton, NJ: Gallup Poll, 1978.

Gill, Brendon. Cited in *Omni Magazine*, August 1988, p. 32.

Gilmore, G. Don. *Angels, Angels, Everywhere*. New York: Pilgrim Press, 1981, p. xi.

Gittner, Louis. *Listen Listen Listen*. Eastsound, WA: The Louis Foundation, 1980, p. 29.

Grayson, David. Cited in Jacob M. Braude, *Braude's Second Encyclopedia of Quotations and Anecdotes*. Englewood Cliffs, NJ: Prentice-Hall, 1957, p. 166.

Greeley, Andrew M. *Angel Fire*. New York: Warner Books, Inc., 1988.

Hill, Napoleon. *Think and Grow Rich*. Greenwich, CT: Fawcett Publications, 1963.

Humann, Harvey. *The Many Faces of Angels*. Marina del Rey, CA: DeVorss and Co., 1986, p. 43.

Huxley, Aldous. *Moksha*. M. Horowitz and C. Palmer (Eds.).

Los Angeles: J.P. Tarcher, Inc., 1977, p. 223.

Jampolsky, Gerald. *Teach Only Love*. Berkeley, CA: Celestial Arts, 1984.

Jeffrey, Francis. *John Lilly, So Far . . . .* Los Angeles: J.P. Tarcher, Inc./St. Martin's Press, 1989.

Jung, Carl G., and Pauli, W. *The Interpretation of Nature and the Psyche. Synchronicity: An Acausal Connecting Principle (C.G. Jung). The Influence of Archetypal Ideas on the Scientific Theories of Kepler (W. Pauli)*. New York: Pantheon Books, 1955.

Krishnamurti, J. "Love, Freedom and Enlightenment." In John White (Ed.), *What Is Enlightenment?* Los Angeles: J.P. Tarcher, Inc., 1984, p. 91.

Long-Chen-Pa. Cited in Barry Stevens, *Burst Out Laughing*. Berkeley, CA: Celestial Arts, 1984, p. 177.

Longfellow, H.W. "Evangeline." Cited in John Bartlett (Ed.), *Bartlett's Quotations*. Boston: Little, Brown and Co., 1955, p. 511.

Maclean, Dorothy. *To Hear the Angels Sing*. Issaquah, WA: Lorian Press. 1987, p. 84.

Milton. "Paradise Lost." Cited in John Bartlett (Ed.), *Bartlett's Quotations*. Boston: Little, Brown and Co., 1955, p. 286.

Neville. *Resurrection*. Marina del Rey, CA: DeVorss and Co., 1966, p. 90.

O'Rell, Max. Cited in Jacob M. Braude, *Braude's Second Encyclopedia of Quotations and Anecdotes*. Englewood Cliffs, NJ: Prentice-Hall, 1957, p. 216.

Pert, Candace. "Each organism has evolved . . ." "Interview." *Omni Magazine*, 1984.

Pert, Candace. "Creativity comes from . . ." Cited in "The Roots of Inspiration," *Omni Magazine*, April 1989, p. 98.

Ponder, Catherine. *The Dynamic Laws of Prosperity*. Marina del Rey, CA: DeVorss and Co., 1985.

Roman, Sanaya. *Spiritual Growth*. Tiburon, CA: H.J. Kramer, Inc., 1989, p. 90.

Sheerin, John. Cited in Kaufman, Daniel. *The Secret of Happiness*. Self-published, n.d., p. 64.

Siegel, Bernie. "The Healing Power of Communicating With Your Body." *East West Journal*, July 1989, p. 76.

Stevens, Barry. *Burst Out Laughing*. Berkeley, CA: Celestial Arts, 1984, p. 75.

Wilbur, Richard. "Love Calls Us to the Things of This World." *Poems of Richard Wilbur*. New York: Harvest, 1963, p. 64.

Dear Reader:

Terry Taylor is collecting angel stories, angel artists, and angel poets for her future book, and for the forthcoming *Angel Newsletter*. Please write if you would like to be included on her mailing list for the newsletter or for the Angel Seminars she offers. Also, feel free to send Terry an angel request, and she will forward it through her angel mailbox. If you would like to schedule an angel conference, please write her for details.

Terry Taylor
Angels Can Fly
P.O. Box 481
Ojai, CA 93024

COMPATIBLE BOOKS ☙ FROM H J KRAMER INC

JOURNEY INTO NATURE
by Michael J. Roads
"If you only read one book this year, make that book *Journey Into Nature*."
— *Friend's Review*

WAY OF THE PEACEFUL WARRIOR
by Dan Millman
Available in book and audio cassette format
A tale of spiritual adventure…a worldwide bestseller!

SEVENFOLD PEACE: BODY, MIND, FAMILY, COMMUNITY, CULTURE, ECOLOGY, GOD
by Gabriel Cousens, M.D.
"This book expands our awareness of the dimensions of peace so that we can all work effectively to create a world at peace." — John Robbins, Author, *Diet for a New America*

An Orin/DaBen Book
OPENING TO CHANNEL: HOW TO CONNECT WITH YOUR GUIDE
by Sanaya Roman and Duane Packer, Ph.D.
This breakthrough book is the first step-by-step guide to the art of channeling.

An Orin/DaBen Book
CREATING MONEY
by Sanaya Roman and Duane Packer, Ph.D.
"To be considered required reading for those who aspire to financial well-being."
— *Body Mind Spirit*

PURE LOVE: AFFIRMATIONS JUST FOR THIS MOMENT
by Carole Daxter
A very special book that affirms our connection to a safe and friendly universe.

LOVE AND PEACE THROUGH AFFIRMATION
by Carole Daxter
"Among the leaders in books that inspire and expand human awareness."
— Colin Sisson, Author, *Rebirthing Made Easy*

TALKING WITH NATURE
by Michael J. Roads
"Reads like a synthesis of *Walden* and *The Secret Life of Plants*." — *East West Journal*

COMPATIBLE BOOKS 🌹 FROM H J KRAMER INC

ORIN BOOKS
by Sanaya Roman
The Earth Life Series is a course in learning to live
with joy, sense energy, and grow spiritually.

LIVING WITH JOY, BOOK I
"I like this book because it describes the way I feel about so many things."
— Virginia Satir, Author, *Peoplemaking*

PERSONAL POWER THROUGH AWARENESS:
A GUIDEBOOK FOR SENSITIVE PEOPLE, BOOK II
"Every sentence contains a pearl..." —Lilias Folan

SPIRITUAL GROWTH: BEING YOUR HIGHER SELF, BOOK III
Orin teaches how to reach upward to align with the higher energies of the universe,
look inward to expand awareness, and move outward in world service.

JOY IN A WOOLLY COAT: GRIEF SUPPORT FOR PET LOSS
by Julie Adams Church
Joy in a Woolly Coat is about living with, loving, and
letting go of treasured animal friends.

EAT FOR HEALTH: FAST AND SIMPLE WAYS OF ELIMINATING
DISEASES WITHOUT MEDICAL ASSISTANCE
by William Manahan, M.D.
"Essential reading and an outstanding selection."— *Library Journal*

YOU THE HEALER: THE WORLD-FAMOUS SILVA METHOD
ON HOW TO HEAL YOURSELF AND OTHERS
by José Silva and Robert B. Stone
You the Healer is the complete course in the Silva Method healing techniques
presented in a do-it-yourself forty-day format.

AMAZING GRAINS: CREATING VEGETARIAN MAIN DISHES
WITH WHOLE GRAINS
by Joanne Saltzman
Amazing Grains is really two books in one, a book of recipes
and a book which teaches the creative process in cooking.